Put the Probe Here

The first (but not the last) Echo book you should read

2nd edition

Christopher Labos MD CM, MSc, FRCP(C)
Chris Lui MD, FRCP(C)

• Dedication •

This book is dedicated to the memory of my dear friend Dr. Chris Lui.

He never got to see our "little project" make it to print, but I have attempted to stay faithful to the vision we planned out together long ago.

I can only hope he will be pleased.

• *Acknowledgements* •

The fact that this book has made it to a second edition is a testament to the many people that have provided me with support and encouragement over the past few years.

Firstly to Anna, who was a great champion of the first edition and who did much to spread the word to many people in and around McGill.

Also to Mr. and Mrs. Lui who, through the MGH Foundation, financially supported this project. Their support has allowed me to keep going and constantly update this work both in print and online.

And finally to the many trainees who read this book and told me it was worthwhile. It was written for you after all.

Table of Contents

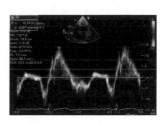

Preface

Dear Reader,

Echocardiography is a critical skill in today's medical landscape. Whether your are in cardiology, internal medicine, intensive care, emergency medicine, anesthesia, a technician or a trainee, echocardiography is proving to be more versatile and more essential with each passing year. Over the next few months (or years as the case may be), you are going to learn a new skill set that will be immensely useful in diagnosing and treating patients. That is, provided you don't rip your hair out first.

Echocardiography requires not only clinical knowledge, but also a certain manual dexterity that is not immediately obvious. Sadly, there is no substitute for practice and you will spend your first months of echo simply learning how to acquire the images and, more likely than not, cursing your inability to get a proper 4-chamber view of the heart.

That is where this handbook comes in. While learning how to perform an echo, one of the major obstacles that there seemed to be was the absence of a simple how-to guide that told us what we needed to know to get through those first frustrating few weeks. How many clips should I be taking and in what order? When should I use CW or PW? When should I use colour? What's that button do? All these are questions that every one of us has had, and is often too embarrassed to ask out loud for fear of looking foolish. Trying to read Catherine Otto's "Textbook of Clinical Echocardiography" or Jae K. Oh's "The Echo Manual" is often too much of an undertaking when you simply want to find out what in God's name is a PISA.

Thus, this book has been written with you in mind, in an attempt to give you the basic outline that we wish we had when we were starting out. It is meant for the person just at the beginning of their echocardiography training. This handbook is not meant to replace any Echo textbook. In fact, most echocardiographers would probably have a fit if they saw to what degree we have attempted to simplify the physics and physiology. Rather, consider it a starting guide, a primer so you can start your first day of your echo rotation ready for work.

We hope you find this guide useful. Learning how to do an echo can be frustrating at first (we know because we were there once too). We hope this guide makes it easier. It was and is a labour or love.

Good luck and happy scanning.

Sincerely,

Christopher Labos MD, CM FRCPC

Chapter 1: Principles of Echo

In this Chapter:
- The physics behind sound propagation
- The concepts of frequency and wavelength and their impact on echo

1.1 Why Echo works: THE PHYSICS OF SOUND PROPAGATION

If you've never really thought about it, sound is really just a disturbance propagating through a material. Your vocal cords vibrate and those vibrations are transmitted through the air to the person sitting across from you who now hears what you are saying. Sound can propagate through any material be it air, water, or yes cardiac muscle. But it must have a material to go through which is why no one can hear Sigourney Weaver scream in space.

Certain tissues transmit sound better than others. Air is particularly bad and solid tissues are much better. The speed of sound in air is 330m/s. It is 1540m/s in the heart itself. Unfortunately, the heart tends to be surrounded by very large air containing structures called lungs that limit the quality of the images that can be achieved. It also limits the number of possible views of the heart that we can get with an echo machine.

We must now, by necessity, do some basic physics because if you understand how sound waves work, you'll understand how echo images are produced. Any wave (be it a sound wave or electromagnetic wave) has three major properties that you need to know. These are velocity, wavelength, and frequency. **Velocity** (v) we have covered already, and it's the speed with which the wave travels through a tissue and is dependent on the type of tissue (slower in air, faster in fluid). The **frequency** is the number of oscillations that the wave produces per second. The unit of frequency (f) is the Hertz (Hz). The human ear can pick up frequencies up to 20 kHz. The piezoelectric crystals of the ultrasound machine can produce sound waves with frequencies of 1.5 MHz up to 7.5 MHz. Since these sound waves are well beyond the human ear's capacity to pick them up, they are referred to as "ultrasound" waves. By now you should be starting to see where the terminology comes from.

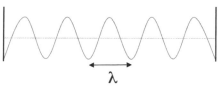

Figure 1.1: Diagram of a sound wave

The final term we need to define is **wavelength** (λ). As the name implies, it is the distance between two cycles in the wave and is related to the other two terms through the following equation:

$$v = f \times \lambda$$

The equation itself is not particularly important for you to remember if you can appreciate that all the properties of the ultrasound wave are interrelated, and if you change one you will affect the others. How this becomes practically relevant, we will address in section 1.3 "Optimizing the image."

1.2 How Echo works: PRODUCING AN ULTRASOUND IMAGE

At first glance, it seems improbable that sound vibrations can be manipulated and used to create reliable two dimensional (and sometimes three dimensional) images. Yet, the ultrasound machine is able to generate sound waves and interpret the properties of the sound waves that come bouncing back.

It all begins with certain special crystals that are at the core of the ultrasound machine. Echo machines work because these crystals are able to transform electricity into sound. These crystals transform electrical oscillations (varying voltages in the electrical current) into mechanical oscillations (which is essentially what makes a sound). The property of these crystals to change electrical oscillations into mechanical oscillations has a specific name: the **piezoelectric** effect. It's also important to note that it's not a one-way phenomenon. Not only do these crystals send out sound waves but they can also receive sound waves and transform them back into electrical oscillations. So on any given cycle, the ultrasound crystals receive an electrical input, transform it into sound waves and then wait. If a sound wave is reflected back, the crystal is distorted and transforms that sound wave into an electrical impulse. That electricity can then be read by a computer and interpreted as an image on a computer screen. Ultrasound crystals can go through this cycle about 1000 times per second. So every millisecond, the crystal will send out a pulse (which lasts about 1 microsecond) and then "listen" for its reflection for the remaining 999 microseconds until it sends out another pulse.

Now you are probably asking what happens to the sound wave once it leaves the transducer. Well if it was travelling through a uniform medium it would continue to travel in a straight line and eventually dissipate. Fortunately, the human body is not a uniform medium. There are many layers with different densities. Every time the sound wave passes through a tissue interface of two different densities, some of the sound wave is reflected back while the piezoelectric crystals eagerly wait for this sound wave reflection or *echo* (get it?). Furthermore, different tissues reflect back different amounts of the sound wave. While bone and other calcified structures reflect back a lot of the wave, blood reflects back very little.

Therefore, two things are being measured when the sound wave is reflected back: the time between the signal impulse and its return (which tells you how deep the structure is) and the intensity of the signal (which tells you how dense the structure is). For example, a high intensity signal reflected back very quickly represents a very superficial and very dense structure, like a rib. The computer will translate these reflective signals into a grey-scale picture so that bone, which is very intense, is displayed as white. Blood, which reflects back a very weak signal, is displayed as black. The heart muscle itself, which reflects back a medium intensity signal, is displayed as varying shades of grey. It will then use the time interval between the sound wave impulse and the sound wave reflections to plot out how deep the structure is and give you the 2 dimensional images you see on your screen.

1.3 Optimizing the image: MAKING ECHO WORK FOR YOU
As you can imagine, and as we've already alluded to, there are a lot of things impeding the sound wave's ability to get to the heart. Skin, muscle, ribs, fat, and breast tissue all reflect back a certain amount of the ultrasound wave and limit your acoustic windows, i.e. the positions where you can get a good view of the heart. Air in the lungs also significantly slows down the transmission of ultrasound waves. Therefore, the standard echo views all involve placing the ultrasound transducer in locations where there is minimal interference from the lungs.

There are however, other ways to optimize the quality of your ultrasound image beyond simply positioning. When you start out, positioning is going to be the major obstacle you must overcome. But, it is important to remember the other factors that may play into image quality.

Earlier, we defined the concepts of velocity, wavelength, frequency and how they related to each other. The wavelength is an important variable because it represents (more or less) the smallest resolution that is possible with ultrasound. In plain English: the shorter the wavelength, the better the resolution. Sadly, with all things in life there is a trade-off. Short wavelengths do no penetrate tissue well. Thus, if you need an ultrasound wave to penetrate deeper into the thoracic cavity you will need a longer wavelength and thus less resolution.

How do you adjust the wavelength? Well you don't. You adjust the frequency (remember how I said all the properties were interrelated). In young thin individuals you can use a relatively high frequency ultrasound wave because that will give you a shorter wavelength and thus better resolution. However, in older obese individuals you will have a lot of subcutaneous fat standing between you and the heart, so you'll need to turn the frequency down to get a higher wavelength that can penetrate deeper through the intervening structures. Will that affect resolution? Absolutely, but that's the price you have to pay.

Although I'm going to try not to repeat myself too often, I will do it here only to remind you that positioning is critically important when you start out. If your first echo images are sub-optimal or even impossible, the first course of action is to move up or down one intercostal space to try to get a better view of the heart. Ribs are going to be your arch nemesis when you first start out, and sadly no amount of fiddling with the properties of the ultrasound waves will get around the problem. That particular skill will come with time and practice.

Before we move on other methods of echo like M-mode and Doppler let's take a moment to summarize what we've learned about basic echocardiography.

- Echocardiography is not witchcraft.
- Piezoelectric crystals are able to transform high frequency changes in electric voltage into ultrasound waves and vice versa.
- Moving between the interfaces of two different media causes some ultrasound waves to be reflected back.
- Different tissues reflect ultrasound waves with different intensities
- The intensity of the ultrasound wave and the delay between impulse generation and reflection allows the computer to create a 2-D grayscale map of the heart and surrounding structures.
- Higher echo frequencies have shorter wavelengths and better resolution but less penetration.
- Lower frequencies with longer wavelengths penetrate deep tissues better but have worse resolution.

Review questions

1. For an obese patient, adequate tissue penetration of the sound wave is achieved by:

   a) increasing the frequency
   b) decreasing the frequency
   c) increasing the wavelength
   d) decreasing the wavelength

2. The quality of echo images is least likely to be affected by:

   a) age
   b) obesity
   c) COPD
   d) body habitus

Chapter 2:
Beyond 2D-other forms of echo

In this Chapter:
- M-Mode echocardiography
- Doppler echocardiography
- The difference between CW and PW
- The principles behind colour and tissue doppler

2.1 M-MODE: A ONE DIMENSIONAL FORM OF ECHO

Up until now we've been talking about two dimensional echocardiography, which is the form of echo that you're probably most familiar with. However, there is another form of echo that predates the 2-D images you see on your screen. That is time-motion or M-mode echocardiography. M-mode is an echo image taken across one single line and then plotted over time. It may be useful, although not entirely accurate and somewhat heretical, to think of 2-D echo as a series of M-mode images summed together. You may wonder why anyone would want to look at a one dimensional image when a two dimensional image is available, but the truth is that the resolution with M-mode is better than with 2-D echo and is especially useful when you want to measure wall thickness and look at (and measure) things that move in the heart (which is essentially everything but especially valves).

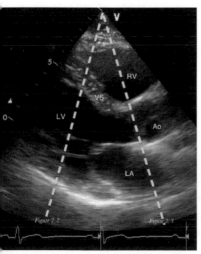

To give you an idea, figure 2.1 shows a typical 2-D echo image with two dashed yellow lines corresponding to figures 2.2 and 2.3. Figure 2.2 shows the left ventricle as it contracts and relaxes in systole and diastole. M-mode through the LV is useful for looking at wall thickness of the ventricle and measuring ventricular cavity size at different phases of the cardiac cycle. Although this would be possible, it would be harder to do with a real time 2-D image. Figure 2.3 shows an M-Mode through the aorta and left atrium. Within the aorta you can see the movement of the aortic valve leaflets.

Figure 2.1: 2-D image of the left ventricle
Ao = aorta LA=left atrium, LV= left ventricle, RV=right ventricle VS=ventricular septum

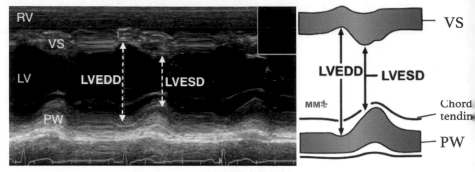

Figure 2.2: M-mode through the LV

LV= left ventricle, RV=right ventricle, PW=posterior wall, VS=ventricular septum, LVEDD=end diastolic diameter, LVESD=end systolic diameter

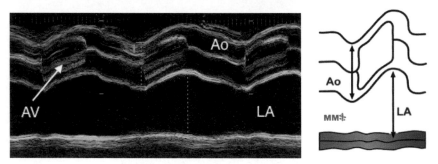

Figure 2.3: M-mode through the Aorta and LA
Ao= aorta, LA=left atrium, AV=aortic valve.

Let's summarize what we've learned about M-mode before moving on to Doppler echocardiography.

- M-mode is a one dimensional section of a 2-D echo image
- M-mode has better resolution than 2-D echo and is particularly useful for measuring wall thickness and looking at the motion of valvular structures.

2.2 DOPPLER ECHOCARDIOGRAPHY

Up until now, we've been talking about ultrasound waves being reflected off various tissues and we've been using blood as one of those tissues. However, blood has many components in it. The major components, of course, are red blood cells and plasma. When ultrasound waves are reflected by red blood cells we get something called the Doppler Effect. The Doppler effect is a change in the frequency of a wave (sound wave, light wave, or whatever other type of wave) due to the motion of the source or the observer. One everyday example that may be helpful is the way a police car siren changes as it approaches you (higher pitch) and then fades after it passes you (lower pitch). In echocardiography, the observer is the echo probe, which is obviously not moving, but the red blood cells are.

For example, let's say the transducer is set to emit an ultrasound wave with a frequency of 2 MHz. If the reflected wave comes back with a frequency higher than 2 MHz then the red blood cells are moving towards the probe. If the frequency reflected back is less than 2 MHz than the red blood cells along the path of the ultrasound wave are moving away from the probe. The computer can actually do one better than telling you whether the red blood cells are moving away or towards the probe; it can actually calculate the speed of these red blood cells using a "simple" formula that is shown below:

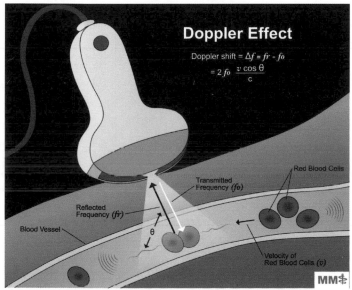

Figure 2.4: The Doppler Effect

I wouldn't worry about memorizing this formula since the echo machine will do the calculations for you. The only important point to take away from it is that the Doppler shift that you measure is dependent upon the angle the ultrasound beam makes with the blood flow that you are measuring. In the diagram above, the ultrasound beam is almost perpendicular to the blood stream. That is actually *not* good because it will cause you to underestimate the true velocity of the blood. The reason for this is pure mathematics. If you remember your high school math days, the cosine of 0 degrees is 1 and the cosine of 90 degrees is 0. So if you are perpendicular to the blood stream (90 degrees), you will get a Doppler shift of zero (which is ridiculous because blood only stops moving when you're dead). As the angle between the ultrasound wave and the blood stream gets progressively bigger, you will progressively underestimate the Doppler shift. Unfortunately, the computer can't correct for this angle because there is no practical way to measure it. The computer will calculate the velocity of blood assuming that the angle is zero and use the following re-arranged formula to calculate the velocity:

$$V = c \times \Delta f / 2fo$$

All that to say, that when using Doppler echocardiography, it is important to line up your ultrasound wave with the flow of blood so that they are parallel to each other as much as possible. **The more you deviate off to an angle, the more you will underestimate the true velocity**.

2.3 PULSE WAVE DOPPLER VS. CONTINUOUS WAVE DOPPLER

There are actually 4 different types of Doppler that are used clinically on a daily basis. The first two are Pulse Wave Doppler (PW) and Continuous Wave Doppler (CW). Colour Doppler and Tissue Doppler we will get to in a minute.

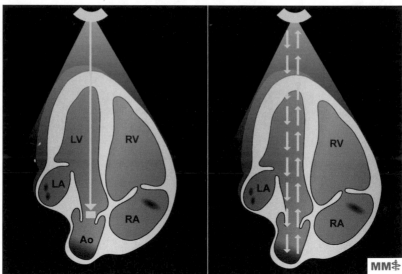

Figure 2.5: Pulse Wave (left) vs. Continuous Wave (right)

The difference is in how the transducer sends out the Doppler signals. In PW, a single transducer crystal sends out a signal at a fixed time interval (called the Pulse Repetition Frequency). In between pulses it waits and "listens" for the signal to be reflected. CW uses two crystals. The signal is sent out by the first crystal but any reflected signals are received by the second crystal. That, way you don't have to wait for the signal to return before sending out another signal and signals can be sent out continuously (hence the name continuous wave Doppler). The diagram to explain these differences can be seen in Figure 2.5 above.

CW is the older of the two forms and probably the easiest to understand. Ultrasound waves are sent out continuously from one crystal and constantly recorded by the second. The main weakness of CW is that you don't know where along the trajectory of the ultrasound waves the Doppler shift was recorded. What you're actually measuring is the *maximum* Doppler shift (and hence the maximum blood velocity) along the path of the ultrasound wave. You might be tempted to think that all blood travels at the same speed, however it doesn't. The most common example is what happens across stenotic valvular lesions where blood velocity increases after the obstruction. Thus if this patient had aortic stenosis you would be measuring maximum blood velocity after the valve, with no way of knowing what the blood velocity was before the valve. If you wanted to know what the blood velocity was before the valve, you would need to use PW.

In PW, you can actually set the Doppler probe to measure the Doppler shift at a specific point (in Figure 2.5 you see it as a green square) which is called the **sample volume**. The sample volume is a point set by the echocardiographer which is a certain distance from the probe. Since the computer knows that distance and since it also knows the velocity of the ultrasound waves, it can figure out how long it will take the ultrasound waves to make it to the sample volume and back again. Then it effectively ignores any signals that are coming in too early or too late, so the only signals it records are the ones from that sample volume.

That may sound too good to be true, and sadly it is. There is unfortunately, one major drawback to PW and it has to do with the single crystal design. Remember that PW uses a single crystal to send and receive the signals. As a result, there is a maximum frequency to the signals that can be sent out (called the **pulse repetition frequency**) because you have to wait for the signals to get back before you can send out another pulse. That means that as you try to interrogate a point further and further away you need to allow more and more time for the reflected signals to make it back, thus you decrease the pulse repetition frequency. You might not think this is such a big deal, but if you decrease the pulse repetition frequency, you are also decreasing the amount of Doppler shift that you can measure. The maximum Doppler shift that you can measure is half the pulse repetition frequency. This number is called the **Nyquist frequency**. Unfortunately, Doppler shifts above the Nyquist frequency then undergo a process called **aliasing**.

To understand aliasing you have to be a fan of old Westerns. In those old movies, if you look carefully, you will sometimes see that the wagon wheels appear to be spinning in the wrong direction. Let's take a moment and imagine a wheel that spins clockwise at one quarter turn per second and that we have a camera that takes a picture every second. In that case you would see something like the diagram in Figure 2.6.

Now imagine that I slowed the camera speed so that it only took a picture every three seconds. The same wheel would now look like the one on the right. In every 3 second interval, the little red ball is making a ¾ turn but since you're only seeing snapshots of its movement it looks like it's making a quarter turn in the *counter-clockwise* direction. This might be a lot to digest in one sitting, but aliasing occurs when something is moving faster then your ability to see or record it. The net result is that it looks like it's moving in the opposite direction.

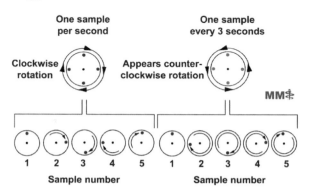

Figure 2.6: an example of aliasing
Modified with permission from echoincontext.edu and Duke University

The same thing occurs with PW. Because of the Nyquist frequency there is a maximum Doppler shift that can be measured. Anything beyond that maximum is measured incorrectly and on the echocardiogram will appear to be going in the opposite direction. To put this in perspective, the Doppler signal might look like blood is going from the aorta into the LV and you might diagnose aortic insufficiency when there isn't any.

Let's take a moment and summarize what we've covered since last time.

- Doppler echocardiography uses the change in frequency of a reflected wave to derive the velocity of moving red blood cells.
- There is Pulsed Wave (PW) and Continuous Wave (CW) Doppler
- PW can measure velocities at a specific point called the sample volume that is set by the echocardiographer.
- PW has a maximum velocity that it can reliably measure. Anything faster than that velocity is subject to aliasing.
- Aliasing makes velocity jets look like they are going in the opposite direction.

- CW cannot measure velocities at a specific point but there is no maximum velocity and thus no aliasing.
- Watching an old western may blow your mind.

Although we've talked about CW and PW there are actually two other forms of Doppler that deserve mention. They are Colour Doppler and Tissue Doppler.

2.4 COLOUR DOPPLER: COLOUR FLOW MAPPING

Colour Doppler is actually based on the principles of PW. What the computer does is actually calculate the blood velocity across a number of points in the area that you select. The velocity is then assigned a colour and intensity. Velocities coming towards the probe are coded red and velocities away from the probe are coded blue. A quick way to remember this is the acronym **BART (blue away, red towards)**. Fast velocities are bright red whereas slower velocities can be more of an orangey red colour. A colour map is usually shown on the echo screen for your convenience. The advantage of colour flow mapping is that it gives you a nice visual way to subjectively appreciate the velocity of the blood flow you're measuring.

2.5 TISSUE DOPPLER

Tissue Doppler is also based on the same principle as PW. Although we've previously always been talking about red blood cells, we can't forget that the heart itself also moves and produces a Doppler effect. By doing a tissue Doppler of the left ventricle you can get a sense of how well it's moving. Although this can be used to look at ventricular contraction, we tend to use it more to look at ventricular relaxation and diastolic dysfunction (but more on that later).

One last summary before we move on to the next chapter:

- There are two additional forms of Doppler echocardiography: colour and tissue Doppler.
- Colour Doppler provides a visual colour coded map of jet velocities.
- Tissue Doppler provides information on the movement of tissue, particularly on diastolic motion of tissue.

Review questions

1. M-mode echocardiography is more useful than 2-D echocardiography for:

   a) measuring pressure gradients
   b) measuring the thickness of walls
   c) measuring velocities
   d) measuring diastolic dysfunction

2. CW would be used rather than PW in which of the following situations:

   a) to measure the maximum velocity across the aortic valve
   b) to measure the velocity at the left ventricular outflow tract
   c) to measure the velocity at the pulmonary veins
   d) to measure the velocity at the hepatic veins

Chapter 3:
Equations you need to know

In this Chapter:
- The Bernoulli Equation
- The Continuity Equation

3.1 THE BERNOULLI EQUATION: CONVERTING VELOCITY INTO PRESSURE

Your eyes may have glazed over as you tried to understand of some the physics behind echocardiography, but here are a couple of things that you really should remember as you start out. We often report pulmonary pressures on an echo and if you didn't know any better you would probably assume there was some way to measure pressure directly. Well... actually there isn't. What you're really measuring is the velocity of blood flow. Every time you use your doppler (whether CW or PW) remember that what you're really measuring is the speed of those red blood cells as they move through the heart. So how do you convert a velocity into a pressure? I'm glad you asked. This is done using the Bernoulli Equation. The actual Bernoulli Equation is quite complicated, but the simplified form is:

$$\Delta P = 4 \cdot V^2$$

Where ΔP is the pressure difference along the path you're measuring, and V is the velocity of blood along that same path.

So if you have a jet of blood that is travelling at 1 m/s, then the pressure gradient generating that jet is 4mmHg. If the speed is 2m/s, then the pressure gradient is 16mmHg. And so on. So let's say that you have tricuspid regurgitation and you see a TR jet going from the right ventricle to the right atrium in systole. Then let's say that you put your Doppler probe on that jet and using CW you measure the max velocity of that jet to be 3m/s. (Remember that if you use PW, you might have problems with aliasing if the jet is too fast. Re-read chapter 2 if that doesn't make sense). That would give you a pressure of 36mmHg according to the Bernoulli equation.

Okay, so what? Well remember some physiology and you'll get your answer. Assuming that the patient has no pulmonic stenosis (which is quite rare except in congenital settings), then RV systolic pressure is the same as pulmonary artery (PA) systolic pressure.

PA systolic pressure = RV systolic pressure

You can then figure out your RV systolic pressure because you've measured the TR jet. If by measuring the TR jet you've found that there is a pressure difference of 36 mmHg between the RV and RA, and if you knew that RA pressure was 3 mmHg, then you could easily deduce that the pressure in the right ventricle (and therefore the pulmonary artery) was 36+3=39 mmHg.

PA systolic pressure = RV systolic pressure

PA systolic pressure = (RV to RA pressure gradient) + RA pressure

By this point, a few of you may have asked how we're supposed to measure RA pressure since I just mentioned there's no way to measure pressures directly. Well, we do that by measuring the IVC in the sub-costal view and looking to see if it collapses or not. Using those two parameters we can estimate what the RA pressure is.

	Normal 3 mm Hg (range 0-5)	Intermediate 8 mmHg (range 5-10)		High 15 mmHg (range 10-20)
IVC diameter	< 21mm	<21 mm	>21mm	>21mm
Inspiratory collapse	> 50%	<50%	>50%	<50%

Table 3.1: How to assess RA pressure

These numbers come from the new American Society of Echocardiography guidelines on assessing the right ventricle and may differ slightly from the numbers you see in other textbooks, but the basic principles are the same. If the IVC is dilated and doesn't collapse with inspiration, then RA pressure is high. (You could also clinically assess RA pressure by looking at the patient's JVP, but this is the echocardiographic way of doing it). Be forewarned though, patients that are intubated or on positive pressure ventilation, may have dilated IVC's without having truly elevated RA pressures.

PA diastolic pressures can be measured using a similar idea. In diastole, since the tricuspid valve is open, RA pressure equals RV pressure. If then there is some PR, then the PA to RV gradient (at end diastole) + RV end-diastolic pressure = PA diastolic pressure. Since the RA and the RV pressures are the same (assuming no tricuspid stenosis) then PA diastolic pressure = PA to RV gradient + RA pressure. That's why when you see any PR you always measure the gradient at end-diastole. A fair number of cavitary pressures can be measured in this way if you remember your physiology. A summary can be found in the following table:

Doppler	Pressure
Peak TR velocity	RV systolic pressure
Peak PR velocity	Mean PA pressure
End-diatolic PR velocity	End-diastolic PA pressure
Peak MR velocity	LA pressure
End-diastolic AR velocity	End-diastolic LV pressure

The Bernoulli equation also has a role beyond the measuring of PA pressures. By measuring blood velocities across valves, you can use the Bernoulli equation to assess the pressure gradient across the valves. High pressure gradients usually imply stenotic valve lesions. For example, if the maximum blood velocity across the aortic valve is 3 m/s, then that means that the maximum pressure gradient across the aortic valve is 36 mmHg (probably representing mild-moderate aortic stenosis). This value is termed the **peak gradient**. The computer will also calculate the average pressure gradient throughout the ejection period and this is termed the **mean gradient**. Physiologically speaking, the mean gradient is the more important of the two and the one that tends to be used clinically. While gradients are always important in assessing valve pathology, they should always be correlated with the valve area and that is done by using the continuity equation, which is coming up next.

3.2 THE CONTINUITY EQUATION: CALCULATING VALVE AREAS

You might be wondering why not simply trace out the valve circumference and have the computer calculate the area rather than bother with complex formulas. Well, you wouldn't be wrong to suggest that and it is done in certain circumstances. But the truth is, it's quite difficult to do in practice and very prone to error. Ultimately, a much easier method is to use the continuity equation which stipulates that the volume of blood flowing into a valve must equal the amount of blood flowing out of a valve. To put that mathematically:

$$Flow\ in = Flow\ out$$

Since cross sectional flow is described as the cross sectional area times the velocity of a fluid moving through that area, the formula becomes.

$$A_1 \times V_1 = A_2 \times V_2$$

Let's take the aortic valve as a practical example. Remember that the inflow of the aortic valve is also the outflow of the left ventricle. So the first thing we measure is the left ventricular outflow tract (LVOT). In the parasternal long axis view, **measure the diameter of the LVOT right at the base where the aortic valve cusps attach** (blue dashed line in figure 3.1). It's usually about 2cm for most people give or take. Assuming that the LVOT is more or less circular, the computer will calculate the area of the LVOT area using πr^2. And now you have A_1.

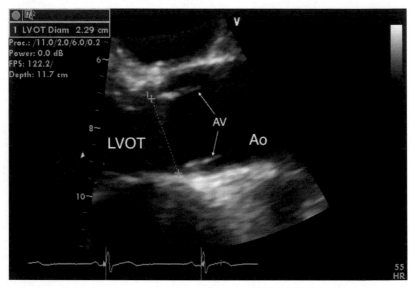

Figure 3.1: How and where to measure the LVOT diameter

Now you need to measure the velocities. This can be accomplished in the apical views, where you also see the LVOT and aortic valves. Why didn't we do this before in the parasternal views? Well remember that to accurately measure velocities, your Doppler probe should be parallel to the velocity jet. In the long axis view, your probe is almost perpendicular to the LVOT and therefore measuring velocities here will be almost useless. So to measure V_1 and V_2 you place your probe along the outflow tract and measure velocities before and after the valve. Remember to use PW for the LVOT velocity before the valve (since you want the velocity at that particular point) [Figure 3.2 left panel] and CW for the aortic velocity after the valve (since you want the maximum velocity after the valve) [Figure 3.2, right panel]. The computer will then calculate your valve area by solving for A_2 where $A2 = A_1 \times V_1/V_2$

It's important to mention one quick point. For these velocities we trace the velocity jets rather than just placing the cursor on the maximum velocity like we do for TR. Why we do that is sort of complicated and maybe not all that important at your level, but here is a brief explanation. In a pulsatile system like your heart, flow velocity varies during an ejection period. It initially starts off slow, speeds up, reaches a maximum and then eventually slows down again until it stops. That's why the Doppler wave has that type of shape. So to truly get a sense of how much is flowing through the valve area in question you need to sum up all these different velocities. That's why we trace the Doppler wave rather than just taking the maximum velocity. If you trace the velocities, you will be giving the computer an area. Mathematically speaking (if you think back to your days of calculus) you're essentially calculating an integral, namely the integral of velocity versus time. That is what we call the **Velocity Time Integral** or VTI, which is a much better representation of the flow across the given cross sectional area. So really the continuity equation should be $A_1 \times VTI_1 = A_2 \times VTI_2$.

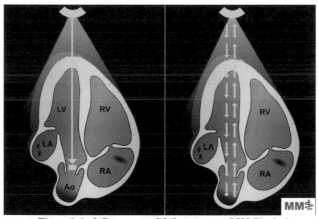

Figure 3.2: Why you use PW to measure LVOT velocity

Let's review what we've seen in this chapter:

- The Bernoulli formula is $\Delta P = 4V^2$ and converts velocity into pressure
- By measuring TR velocities, we can use the Bernoulli equation to measure the RV-RA pressure gradient.
- By adding RA pressure to RV-RA pressure gradient, we can estimate PA systolic pressure (assuming no pulmonic stenosis).
- The Bernoulli equation can also be used to measure pressure gradients across valves and identify valve stenosis.
- The continuity equation is: A1 x V1 = A2 x V2
- By measuring LVOT diameter and the Doppler velocities before and after the aortic valve, we can measure aortic valve area.

Review questions

1. If the maximum TR velocity is 2m/s and the IVC is small and
   collapses with inspiration, then the PA systolic pressure is:
   - a) 19 mmHg
   - b) 24 mmHg
   - c) 29 mmHg
   - d) 34 mmHg

2. Estimations of PA systolic pressure are invalid if there is:
   - a) Heart failure
   - b) Mitral stenosis
   - c) Pulmonic stenosis
   - d) Atrial septal defect

3. Which of the following is true when measuring velocities for the
   continuity equation in the calculation of aortic valve area:
   - a) Measure V1 with PW and V2 with CW
   - b) Measure V1 with CW and V2 with CW
   - c) Measure V1 with PW and V2 with PW
   - d) Measure V1 with PW and V2 with PW

Chapter 4: The Views

<u>In this Chapter:</u>
- Reviewing the 5 standard views of the transthoracic echocardiogram
- Parasternal long axis
- Parasternal short axis
- Apical
- Subcostal
- Suprasternal

Up until now, we've been talking mainly about the theory of performing an echo. Now we're going to start getting practical. One of the first questions everyone asks is, "Where do I put the echo probe?"

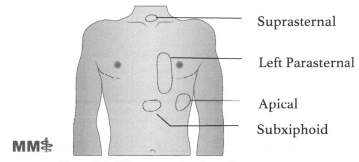

Figure 4.1: Where to put the echo probe

There are certain standard views that offer the best quality images. Remember that sound waves do not travel well through air and the lungs are full of the stuff. So placing the probe randomly on the chest will not be particularly useful. The trick becomes in finding locations where the heart is close to the surface without much lung tissue in the way. Those views are listed here.

4.1 PARASTERNAL LONG AXIS VIEW

Most of the exam is done with the patient lying on their left side with their left arm tucked under their head. The parasternal views usually involve placing the probe just lateral to the sternum at around the 3rd or 4th intercostal space. Often one has to check one intercostal space above or below to see which view provides the best "window" or view of the heart. The light on the probe should point towards the right shoulder. This will provide a cross section of the heart going from the right shoulder to the spleen. The typical image will look like this:

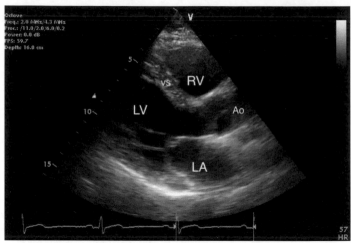

Figure 4.2: the parasternal long axis

LA= left atrium, LV = left ventricle, Ao = aorta, PW = posterior wall, VS = ventricular septum, RV = right ventricle.

Without moving the probe very much you can get images of the RV inflow (i.e. the right atrium and right ventricle) and the RV outflow (i.e. the right ventricle and pulmonary artery). You simply need to angle the probe slightly toward the sternum (medially for those of you who need fancy terms) to get the right atrium and right ventricle lined up as you see below:

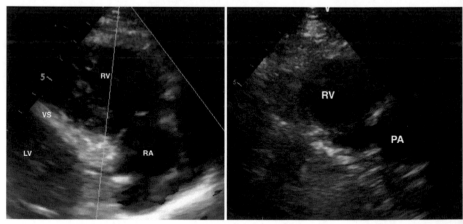

Figure 4.3: RV inflow (left) and RV outflow (right) from the parasternal view

LV = left ventricle, VS = ventricular septum, RA=right atrium, RV = right ventricle, PA=pulmonary artery.

By moving the probe the other way (i.e. away from the sternum), you get the RV outflow view with the right ventricle emptying into the pulmonary artery.

4.2 PARASTERNAL SHORT AXIS VIEW

Moving from the long axis to the short axis view is really easy. Simply rotate the probe by 90 degrees so that now the light is pointing towards the left shoulder as opposed to the right. Now the plane of the echo image has shifted by 90 degrees as well, essentially cutting the heart in cross-section to produce a series of doughnut shapes. Examples are shown below:

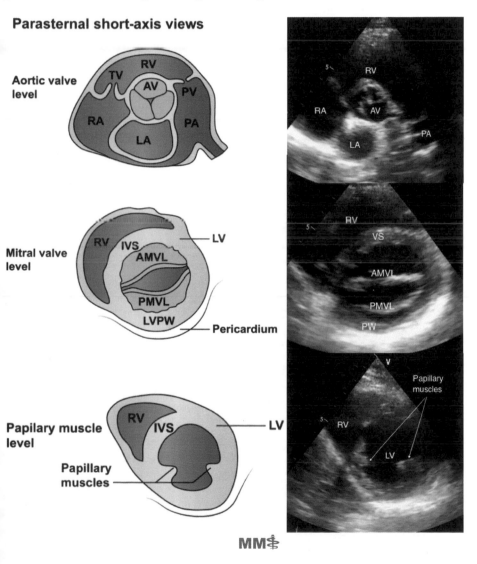

Figure 4.4: the parasternal short axis

By angling the probe superiorly, the aortic valve comes into view (Figure 4.4, top). As the probe is angled downwards, the mitral valve with its typical "fishmouth" appearance comes into view (Figure 4.4 middle). Further angling downwards will show us the papillary muscles (the posteromedial and anterolateral as they are so creatively called, Figure 4.4 bottom). Finally, at the most extreme cut the LV apex can be visualized. [Most purists will tell you that you can't really see the LV apex from the short axis view and that what you're really seeing is just an extremely angular cut of the left ventricle, however for your purposes it's close enough].

4.3 APICAL VIEW

Up until now, we haven't really moved the probe at all since we started the exam. We've angled it up and down and rotated it by 90 degrees to get the short axis view. Now for the first time, we're actually going to move the probe to get the apical 4-chamber view. We get this view by placing the probe on none other but the apex of the heart with the light pointing down.

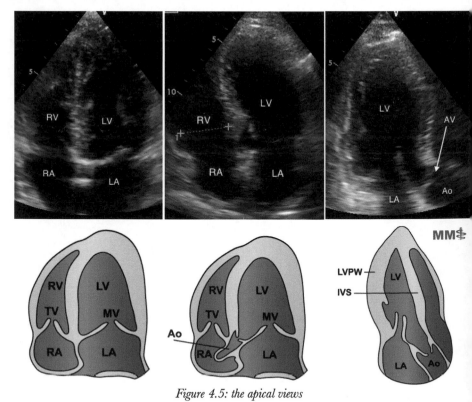

Figure 4.5: the apical views

If you orient the probe with the light pointing up, you will simply get a mirror image of the original picture. With the probe pointing down, the right sided chambers are on the left and the left sided chambers are on the right. While most people do it this way, at the Mayo Clinic they like doing it reversed and so the light points up and the right sided chambers appear on the right.

Getting a good apical view is quite challenging, and most people when they start off in echocardiography place the probe too high and get a rather oddly angled image of the heart which is often referred to as the "resident's 4 chamber view." To avoid being the target of this traditional ridicule there is one trick you can try. Palpate the patient's precordium and feel for the point of maximal impulse (PMI). Placing your probe on the PMI is your best shot at getting good quality images from the apical position.

The standard apical 4-chamber view shows the four chambers of the heart nicely aligned as shown in Figure 4.5 left. With a small clockwise rotation of the probe (and an even slighter tilting of the probe anteriorly), the aortic root is brought into a view and we get the 5 chamber view (the aorta is considered the 5th chamber, Figure 4.5 middle). By rotating the probe a little more, the right sided chambers are lost and we get the LA, LV and aorta lined up in what is essentially a sideways view of the parasternal long axis view we started with. This view is called the long axis or 3-chambered view Figure 4.5, right).

4.4 SUBXIPHOID OR SUBCOSTAL VIEW

At this point, the patient has been lying on his left side since the exam began and his or her arm is probably numb. Now you can ask the patient to turn on his or her back which they will gratefully do. The probe is now placed just under the diagram with the light pointing towards the patient's right. If you have the light pointing to the patient's left, you will simply get a mirror image of what you would have otherwise gotten. Again, neither one is actually right or wrong. It's simply a matter of convention. The typical long axis of the subcostal view is seen in Figure 4.6.

You will probably notice that this view is very much like the apical 4 chamber view, except that it is sideways. For this reason, the subcostal can be particularly useful in patients who do not have good images in the parasternal or apical views for whatever reason (ex. intubated, COPD, etc.) It is also pretty much the only view where you will get a good look at the atrial septum and can look for any septal defects.

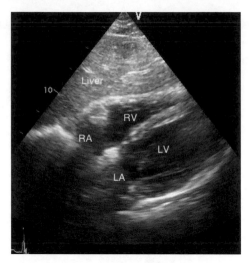

Figure 4.6: subcostal view

If you now rotate the probe by 90 degrees you will get the subcostal short axis view, which again is very much like the parasternal short axis view and allows us to see the aortic valve as well as a number of cross-sectional cuts through the LV.

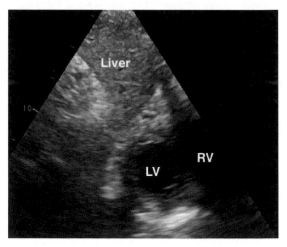

Figure 4.7: the subcostal short axis view

Finally, we can use the subcostal view to look at the major vessels, namely the IVC and aorta. By angling the probe towards the patient's right, we will see the liver, the hepatic veins draining into the IVC, and the IVC draining into the right atrium.

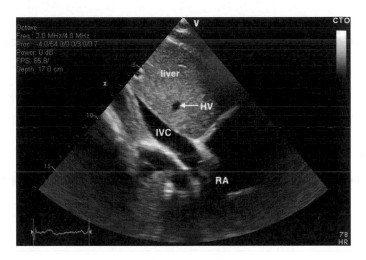

Figure 4.8: IVC seen in the subcostal view
HV= hepatic vein, IVC= inferior vena cava

This view is particularly important for a couple of reasons. First, it allows us to measure the IVC and estimate RA pressure (which we need to calculate pulmonary artery pressure). Secondly, It allows us to Doppler the hepatic veins which is essential to diagnosing things like constrictive pericarditis.

Finally, by angling the probe back towards the left we can see the abdominal aorta.

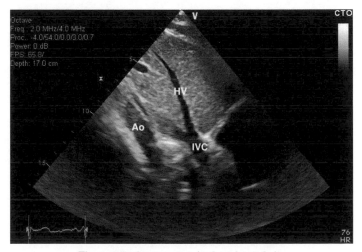

Figure 4.9: the aorta seen in the subcostal view
HV= hepatic vein, IVC= inferior vena cava

Although it is rookie mistake to confuse the abdominal aorta and the IVC (I've done it myself), a few key differences between the two structures should help you keep them straight. The aorta is a pulsatile vessel and has thick walls, while the IVC is non-pulsatile with the thin walls that characterize veins. The IVC usually collapses (but obviously won't with high RA pressures). Also, the IVC feeds into the right atrium, while the aorta obviously does not. Finally, by applying colour Doppler to the structure in question you can tell whether the blood is coming towards you (which means it's the aorta) or going away from you (which means it's the IVC). Some people consider this last point as cheating since you should be able to tell them apart without having to use Doppler but I figure you should have all the tools at your disposal.

4.5 SUPRASTERNAL VIEW

The last view of the transthoracic echo exam is the suprasternal view. As the name suggests it involves placing the probe in the suprasternal notch with the light pointing towards the patient's chin. Angling down and slightly towards the patient's left will give you perhaps your only view of the descending thoracic aorta. In theory, you should see the ascending, arch, and descending aorta (with the PA running under the arch), but in practice usually only the descending with a hint of the arch is visible.

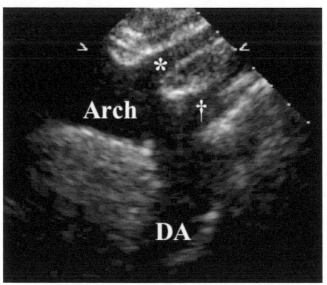

Figure 4.10: The aortic arch in the suprasternal view
DA=Descending aorta, *= left carotid, †=left subclavian

By rotating the probe 90 degrees, you will get the short-axis suprasternal view which is sometimes called the spider view. It's been given that name because the left atrium with the always elusive pulmonary veins feeding into it kind of looks like a big spider with four little legs. Of course spiders are supposed to have eight legs but that's not important right now. While you may be able to see one or possibly two pulmonary veins in the apical view, the spider view is the only time you might be able to see all four on a transthoracic echo (you will often need transesophageal to look at the pulmonary veins).

Apart from looking at the pulmonary veins, you can also see the arch in cross section and a longitudinal view of the right pulmonary artery. Although theoretically easy, it can be a challenging view to get. It may even be impossible in a large number of people. It is often not done as part of a routine echo.

Finally, the textbooks will tell you that you can angulate the probe to the right to see the SVC. Again, while possible in thin, young, and exceptionally echogenic people it will be next to impossible in most elderly and slightly overweight patients of an adult cardiology practice. If you manage to image the SVC, give me a call and I will buy you a steak dinner.

Let's review what we've seen in this chapter:

- There are 5 basic views in the transthoracic echocardiogram:
  - o   parasternal long axis
  - o   parasternal short axis
  - o   apical
  - o   subcostal
  - o   suprasternal

- There's no substitute for practice. Reading this chapter is not enough.

Review questions

1. Achieving a good 4-chamber view is more likely when the probe is placed:
   a) Just under the left nipple
   b) Over the PMI
   c) At the 5th intercostal space
   d) At the axilla

2. The suprasternal view is primarily used for looking at the:

   a) Left ventricle
   b) Right ventricle
   c) Aorta
   d) Pulmonary veins

3. The subcostal view can be used to view all the following except:

   a) IVC
   b) Abdominal aorta
   c) Right ventricle
   d) Pulmonary veins

Chapter 5: The Step by Step Guide to Doing an Echo

In this Chapter:
- An ordered approach to performing the routine transthoracic echo
- What to look for and measure on each clip

Note: What follows is a suggested approach and you will encounter minor variations from one laboratory to another in the way things are done. Although it doesn't really matter in what order you do things, you may wish to follow whatever the routine is for any given lab to avoid the incessant whining and hissing of cardiologists – it can be so irritating.

Parasternal Long Axis:

Probe placed at left sternal border with the light pointing towards the right shoulder.

Clip 1: Basic parasternal long axis view.
Make sure the depth is adjusted so that the posterior wall and the descending aorta (seen in circular cross section beneath the AV groove) are clearly visible and any posterior effusions (pericardial and/or left pleural effusion) will be appreciated (pleural effusions lie posterior to the aorta while pericardial effusions are anterior to it). Record 4 cycles for the clip.

Clip 2: Zoom on the mitral valve.
Press "HR Zoom" and move the trackball to position your window over the mitral valve. Make sure both the mitral annulus and the leaflets are visible within the window. Look for abnormalities in leaflet structure such as thickening, prolapse or a rheumatic "hockey stick" mitral valve of MS.

Clip 3: Colour zoom on mitral valve
Press the colour button to place colour on the zoomed view of the mitral valve. Look for mitral regurgitation.

Clip 4: Zoom on the aortic valve.
Move the zoom window to look at the aortic valve leaflets (the most anterior cusp is the right coronary cusp, the more posterior cusp is the non-coronary cusp; the left cusp is not seen in this view). Look for thickening, calcification and mobility of the valve. Reduced mobility raises the possibility of aortic stenosis however this diagnosis cannot be made by this observation alone.

Clip 5: Colour zoom on aortic valve
Place colour on the zoomed view of the aortic valve. Look for aortic regurgitation appearing below the valve in diastole.

Clip 6: Measure the diameter of the left ventricular outflow tract (LVOT)
While still on the zoomed view of the aortic valve, measure the LVOT diameter. Press the menu button and from *Dimension,* select LVOT. Using the track ball, position the cursor at the base of the right coronary cusp where the anterior aortic root and interventricular septum meet, click and then move the cursor to the base of the non-coronary cusp at its junction with the base of the anterior mitral leaflet and click again.

> The LVOT diameter is a crucial and it should always be measured on a zoomed view. Why? Because many formulas used in echo (see chapter 3) involve squaring the LVOT diameter and any error made during this measurement, will also be squared!

Clip 7: Measure Aortic dimensions
The aortic root is measured routinely at three different levels: at the level of the sinuses of Valsalva, sino-tubular junction, and proximal ascending aorta. Often minor adjustments in the position of the probe are necessary to see all three simultaneously. This assessment may be performed either in the zoomed or more commonly the standard parasternal long axis view. Select *Aorta* from the measurement menu. The diameter at the level of the **sinuses of Valsalva** is measured at the largest point right after the aortic valve leaflets, the **sino-tubular junction** at the level where the aorta narrows slightly above the sinuses of Valsalva, and **ascending aorta** at one or more levels above the sino-tubular junction. In so far as possible, care must be taken to assure that the aorta appears as a symmetric structure. If it appears asymmetric, e.g. one sinus or Valsalva is bigger or more prominent than the other or one aortic wall looks thicker than the other, then chances are you are not positioned properly to make the necessary measurements.

Clip 8: M-mode of Ao/LA.
Return to 2D view and use the trackball to position the cursor (if no line is seen on the screen press the "Cursor" button) and adjust its position so that it crosses through the aorta at the level of the aortic valve and left atrium, then press the M-mode button. Select Ao/LA study (under the Dimension menu) and measure the aortic diameter at end-diastole (i.e. right over the QRS complex) and then measure the widest left atrial diameter posterior to the aortic root.

Clip 9: LA diameter

Return to 2D view (push the M-mode button again to turn it off) and measure the largest LA diameter using the two-dimensional image, ideally along the same axis that you measured in M-mode. This measurement is found under *Volume* in the measurement menu and is labeled "D1." "D1" is the antero-posterior diameter of the left atrium – you will encounter "D2" – the medial-lateral dimension, and "D3" – the supero-inferior dimension, when you get to the apical views described below. These dimensions are used to calculate left atrial volume – don't worry the software will do the math.

Not sure where the posterior left atrial wall is? Sometimes it is difficult to know exactly where the posterior left atrial wall resides and everything looks a bit fuzzy back there due to the fact that the pulmonary veins make holes in the wall you're trying to find. Try locating the brightest echo behind the left ventricle and follow that echo as it extends behind the left atrium – this bright echo is the pericardial reflection and will be contiguous with the posterior left atrial wall. Sort of like following a trail of breadcrumbs...

Clip 10: M-mode of LV.

Return to 2D view and drop a cursor (just like you did above for the aorta and left atrium) through the LV at the level of the tips of the mitral valve leaflets, then switch to M-mode. Under the Dimension menu, select "LV study". Measure the septal thickness, end-diastolic diameter, and posterior wall thickness all in a straight line just over the QRS complex. Then measure end-systolic diameter at the narrowest portion. Relatively straight forward right? Maybe - but measurements of septal and posterior wall thickness are not necessarily that easy as it is often difficult to determine just where to put your cursor since you might end up accidentally measuring papillary muscles or portions of the valve apparatus.

Clip 11: RV inflow

Return to 2D parasternal long axis view and angulate the probe medially and towards a point somewhere between the patient's right hip and right foot. Minor degrees of probe rotation either clockwise or counter clockwise may make the pictures look more like those in the books. Clip a good view of the RA, tricuspid valve, and RV.

Clip 12: Colour of RV inflow

Place colour on the RV inflow clip. Look for TR. Some degree of tricuspid regurgitation is present in 60 – 80% of normal hearts. Colour flow imaging in this view commonly detects flow returning to the right atrium from the IVC (often seen as a circular appearing structure entering the right atrium at the lower left part of the image).

Clip 13: Doppler measurement of TR.

With the colour flow view of the RV inflow still on, press the cursor button and align the cursor parallel through the TR jet and then press the CW button. Adjust the "baseline" and "scale" knobs so that the spectral Doppler signal appears in its entirety on the monitor. When you are happy with the appearance of the spectral flow signal i.e. you have the complete spectral envelope not just part of it, press the "Freeze" button. Measure the "TR max" (found in the Tricuspid menu) by positioning the cursor over the apex of the spectral Doppler curve and clicking. Not so hard is it? Well, sometimes not so easy either. Some things to keep in mind: Tricuspid regurgitant jets are often eccentric rather than central making obtaining good spectral tracings problematic. The jet may be better examined from other views such as the four chamber view or the parasternal short axis view as outlined below. In addition, you probably noted that there was considerable respiratory variation in "TR max" with velocities being higher in inspiration than in expiration. The presence of extrasystoles or irregular rhythms of any description may also result in significant variation. Convention varies as to what to do here. In the absence of rhythm problems some choose to use either inspiration or an average of inspiration or expiration beats while others choose to make the measurement in held mid respiration. With very irregular rhythms (most notably atrial fibrillation) there is little choice but to average a number of beats. With isolated ectopy the TR max from both the ectopic beat and the first post ectopic beat should not be measured.

Clip 14: RV Outflow

Go back to the 2D view and angulate the probe laterally and toward a point between the head and left shoulder. Again you may need to rotate the probe slightly one way or another to get a decent picture and this is one of the more technically challenging views to get with consistency. This view shows the right ventricular outflow tract below the pulmonic valve, the pulmonic valve and the proximal portion of the main pulmonary artery above the pulmonic valve. Clip a good view of the RV outflow tract, pulmonic valve, and pulmonary artery.

Clip 15: Colour of RV Outflow

Press the colour button to place colour on the RV outflow clip. Look for pulmonary regurgitation and any evidence of flow disturbance at or above the pulmonary valve. As was the case for the tricuspid valve, pulmonary regurgitation is very common in normal hearts.

Clip 16: Doppler measurement of Pulmonary Flow.

Press the cursor button, align the cursor across the right ventricular outflow tract and then press the CW button. You now have a spectral display of flow across the RV outflow tract. Position the baseline so that both diastolic (which will appear above the baseline) and systolic flow (which will appear below the baseline) is seen on the screen and use the scale knob to adjust the size. From the measurement menus select "PV max" from the <u>Pulmonic</u> menu and place the cursor at the tip (bottom) of the systolic flow signal. Sometimes pulmonary systolic velocities are traced as well. Make sure there is no significant RV to PA gradient (a velocity above 2 m/s) that would suggest PS. Then select "PRend Vmax" and measure pulmonary regurgitation if any is present. Measure the jet above the baseline at end diastole.

Parasternal Short Axis:

Return to the parasternal long axis view. Now rotate the probe 90 degrees clockwise so that the light points towards the patients left shoulder. Center the aortic valve in the window.

Clip 17: Aortic valve
Adjust the probe so that all 3 leaflets are visible and the valve and the base of the aortic root appear as a concentric circle. Also ensure that the right atrium, tricuspid valve, RV and contiguous RVOT, pulmonic valve, and PA can be seen arching around the top of the aortic valve from left to right on the monitor. Clip a view of these structures.

Clip 18: Zoom on Aortic Valve.
Press "HR Zoom" and move the trackball to position your window so that the entire aortic valve is seen. Examine the structure and mobility of the aortic valve. In this view the anterior most leaflet is the right coronary cusp, the non coronary cusp will appear below it and slightly to your left while the left coronary cusp is below and slightly to your right. The opening of the normal aortic valve appears as an inverted triangle. Make sure there are three separate cusps that open and move separately from one another. Bicuspid valves obviously have only two cusps. Sometimes the distinction between tricuspid and bicuspid valves can be made, not by counting cusps, but by observing how the valve opens. A bicuspid valve has a variably oriented, elongated oval opening rather than a triangular one. Examine the leaflets and leaflet commissures for structural changes such as fusion, thickening or calcification. Clip a view that best demonstrates any abnormality present.

Clip 19: Colour on Aortic Valve
Push the Colour button. Look for evidence of turbulent flow through the valve in systole or aortic regurgitation in diastole. If aortic regurgitation is present, it is important to make sure you align the image so that both the valve leaflets and the regurgitant jet are seen at the same time.

Clip 20: Colour on RV inflow
Place colour on RV inflow - look for any TR

Clip 21: Doppler measurement of TR
CW Doppler of RV inflow – if tricuspid regurgitation is present "TR Max" should again be measured in the manner as described in Clip 13 above. Because of the variability in jet orientation, such jets should be measured from a number of different views and the view that yields the best spectral Doppler pattern and the highest velocity used for any required calculations.

Clip 22: Colour on RV outflow
Place colour on RV outflow – look for any PR.

Clip 23: Doppler measure of Pulmonary Flow
CW Doppler of RV outflow – measure "PVmax" and any PR (at end diastole) as described previously in Clip 16. As previously described, the principle of interrogating jets from different views is to be sure you don't miss a significant abnormality that wasn't seen in a previous view and also to ensure that Doppler flow data are both accurate and reproducible.

Clip 24: Short axis of Mitral valve
To obtain the short axis view of the mitral valve from the parasternal short axis of the aortic valve, angulate the probe very slightly towards the patient's left and inferiorly until the mitral valve comes into view. Both the anterior and posterior leaflets should now be visible as well as the medial and lateral commissures of the mitral valve. Obtaining the best picture often requires slight clockwise or counter clockwise rotation of the probe until all aspects of the valve are visible. Again as you did in the parasternal long axis view of the mitral valve, examine the leaflets for any areas of thickening or irregularity and look at the commissures for evidence of fusion suggestive of rheumatic valve disease. The short axis view of the mitral valve allows you to examine the valve leaflets in a medial – lateral orientation. Push the Colour button and look for evidence of mitral regurgitation in the same way as you looked for aortic regurgitation with the aortic valve described above. Last but not least, the mitral valve is at the base of the left ventricular myocardium – observe the contraction pattern at this level. Clip views of the mitral valve with both the Colour on and off.

Clip 25: Short axis of Papillary muscles
Continued slight angulation inferiorly and to the patients left from the short axis view of the mitral valve will bring the papillary muscles into view with the posteromedial papillary muscle to the left and the anterolateral on the

right. Adjust your imaging plane such that the papillary muscles appear to be relatively symmetric within the ventricular cavity. This view is also known as the mid ventricular level and is used to assess left ventricular systolic function and delineate segmental wall motion abnormalities. Clip a view.

Clip 26: Short Axis of Apex
Continued angulation inferiorly and to the left will bring you to the apex (or something that looks like it might be the apex). In reality, this usually produces a foreshortened and oblique view of this structure however beauty as they say is in the eye of the beholder. A more accurate view of the apex can sometimes be obtained by dragging the probe from the papillary muscle view down an interspace and posteriorly with slight rotation one way or the other towards the apical impulse you felt with your fingers (you did feel for the apical beat didn't you?). The true ventricular apex is usually much more posterior than is generally appreciated. Once you've found it (if you find it) observe its size and contraction pattern. Clip a view.

Apical 4 chamber:
Move the probe to the apex with the light pointing down (it's best to place the probe where you feel the PMI – fingers work best here). You will also likely need to increase the depth a little.

Clip 27: Standard 4 chamber view
Make sure the LA, RA, RV and LV are all visible. This is often a difficult view to get. Make sure that you're not seeing any of the aorta or aortic valve in the picture – if you do, you're angled too far anteriorly and you need to angle more posteriorly. Often rotating the probe a few degrees one way or the other will help. You will make various measurements here as described below but for the moment just look at the general size of the chambers, and the contraction pattern of the left and right ventricles and the motion patterns of the mitral and tricuspid valves. The lateral wall (to your right) and septum (to your left) are the left ventricular walls you see here. When you're happy with your image, clip a view.

Clip 28: Colour of RV inflow
Place colour on tricuspid valve (you remember how to do that now don't you?) – and focus on the tricuspid valve. The leaflets you see in this view are the anterior and septal leaflets. Look for tricuspid regurgitation and if present, note the direction of the regurgitant jet. Clip a view.

Clip 29: Doppler Measurement of TR
Use the CW Doppler and measure TR Max as previously outlined above. You will probably have discerned by now that we measure parameters from more than one view. The principle here is that jets are often eccentric rather

than central and may be seen better in one view than in another – remember you want to be as parallel to the jet as possible when making these measurements. When it comes to quantification of lesions, it is important to use multiple views. This is particularly true of lesions like tricuspid or mitral regurgitation and aortic stenosis. One picks the best flow envelope with the highest velocity to use in quantitative analysis. Clip a view when things are picture perfect.

Clip 30: Measure RV size
Conventionally on the routine examination, the right ventricle is measured only in diastole (you will learn how to make additional measurements at a later date). Measurements are made at two separate sites: the mid portion of the right ventricle at or just distal to the tips of the tricuspid valve and at the base, at or just beneath the tricuspid annulus. The best way to accomplish this task is to press the "Freeze" button and than use the trackball to move through the frames until you find one just before the tricuspid valve begins to close. Once you've found that frame, click the "Calliper" button and make the required measurements. When you're done and with both the measurements still on the screen, clip a view for posterity.

Clip 31: Measure LA and RA size
Recall that you previously measured the left atrium from the parasternal long axis view. What you measured there was the anteroposterior diameter of the left atrium also known as D1. Now we are going to measure the medial-lateral dimension (known as D2) and the superior-inferior dimension of the left atrium (known as D3). From the measurement menu choose "volume" and than "left atrium". You will see that D1 already has a value entered from your measurement in the parasternal long axis view. Click on either D2 or D3 to begin recording these measurements. Both measurements are made at the end of systole when the atrium is generally largest. The medial-lateral dimension (D2) is made at the mid portion of the left atrium and extends from the lateral wall to the atrial septum. The superior-inferior dimension (D3) extends in a straight line from the center point of the mitral annulus to the top of the left atrium. Be careful that your line does not go below the mitral annulus otherwise you will be including a portion of the left ventricle as part of the atrium. Why all these measurements of the left atrium? Well, first it allows calculation of left atrial volume (relax, the machine does it automatically) which is a more useful marker to follow in patients with mitral regurgitation and other disease states. Also, just measuring D1 can be problematic because sometimes it can be normal even in the presence of significant left atrial enlargement – this occurs roughly 15% of the time.

Now, on to the right atrium! From the measurement menu choose "Dimension" and then "Right atrium". Measure the medial-lateral dimension and superior-inferior dimensions of the right atrium in the same fashion as you did for the left atrium. These are generally the only measurements we make of the right atrium during the routine examination and they don't have fancy letter designations like the left atrium does.

Measurements of both the left and right atrium in the four-chamber view are generally made at the same time on the same image. Once you have completed your measurements, clip a view to record your meticulous work for posterity.

Clip 32: Colour on Mitral valve
Push the colour button and focus on the mitral valve and left ventricular inflow tract. Look for mitral regurgitation – if present, make a mental note of the direction of the regurgitant jet. Clip a view of your colourful image.

Clip 33: PW Doppler of Mitral inflow
Place the cursor along the path of mitral inflow with the sample volume (the little box on the cursor) at the tips of the mitral leaflets. Push the PW button and adjust the baseline of the resultant spectral Doppler tracing downwards so the tracing of mitral inflow appears in its entirety on the screen. The spectral tracing should look a little bit like the letter "M" with the first peak called the E wave representing rapid ventricular filling and the second peak or A wave representing atrial contraction at the end of diastole just after the P wave of the ECG lead. Press the measurement button, then Mitral Valve and then select the appropriate submenu to measure the peak E wave, the deceleration time (slope from E wave peak to baseline) and A wave. These values are used in the assessment of diastolic left ventricular function which you will learn more about later on.

Apical 5 Chamber View:
Angulate the probe slightly upwards with a slight clockwise rotation until the aortic valve and proximal aorta come into view.

Clip 34: Colour on Aortic Valve
Place colour on aortic valve and LVOT – look for any evidence of accelerated flow along the left ventricular outflow tract during systole and for aortic regurgitation during diastole.

Clip 35: Measure LVOT velocity (V1)
Press the PW button to turn on PW Doppler and then the Measurement button. Under the "Aortic" section of the measurements, click on LVOT. Now use the track ball to position the cursor about one centimeter proximal to the aortic valve (ideally at the same level where you measured the LVOT diameter) and adjust the baseline so that the spectral tracing looks

symmetric. When you have three or four satisfactory looking beats push "Freeze" to freeze your image. Now using the trackball, trace one of your spectral samples and then move the cursor to the next spectral sample along the baseline and click again – this latter maneuver allows the machine to calculate the R-R interval and subsequently other types of quantitative measurements. Clip your screen and measurements to save an example for posterity.

Clip 36: Measure aortic valve velocity (V2)
Press the "CW" button and align the cursor with the trackball so that it crosses the left ventricular outflow tract, the aortic valve and the proximal part of the ascending aorta. Adjust the baseline so that the resulting spectral flow pattern is completely displayed and freeze the screen when you have a few nice looking beats. Unless you have changed the measurement menu after recording the LVOT velocity, you should not have to make further adjustments as turning the CW on will cause it to default to aortic velocity (V2). Now trace one or two of the resulting spectral flows in the same fashion as you did for the LVOT velocity. The computer will automatically generate peak and mean pressures as well as an aortic valve area if you previously measured the LVOT diameter. When you're done, clip the screen with your measurements. Keep in mind that measurements made for both LVOT and aortic velocities in patients with frequent ectopic beats should not be made on the flow resulting from the ectopic beat or the post-extrasystolic beat as these will yield velocities that may be too low or too high respectively. Patients with atrial fibrillation leave you no choice but to trace a number of beats from which the computer will generate average values.

Clip 37: Pulmonary veins
Return to the standard four chamber view as a starting point, press the "Colour" button and look in the superior portion of the left atrium for a pulmonary vein. These are usually evident as small red jets in systole and diastole entering the left atrium near its wall. The right upper pulmonary vein is usually the easiest to find as it enters the left atrium near the superior portion of the interatrial septum. If you have trouble finding a pulmonary vein, try angling or rotating the probe very slightly one way or another. Clip an example of your best guess for a pulmonary vein.
Clip 38: Doppler of Pulmonary veins
Once you've found a pulmonary vein, press "PW" and position the sample volume (the little box on the cursor) in a portion of the pulmonary vein that is outside the left atrium and left atrial wall. Adjust the baseline so that the resultant spectral flow pattern looks pretty. You will see pulmonary venous flow during both systole and diastole called respectively "S" and "D" waves

that appear above the baseline and an "A" wave representing atrial contraction below the baseline. The height of these waves as well as the duration in some cases is useful in assessing the various degrees of diastolic dysfunction. If you have been skilful or fortunate enough to find anything that vaguely represents what is described above, by all means clip an example. If you've managed to record all of these waves (subject to verification), you will receive a gold star and the rest of the day off. Examination of the pulmonary veins is challenging even for the technically adept.

Clip 39: Tissue Doppler
Velocity of the mitral annulus in the four-chamber view is the most frequently used type of Tissue Doppler measurement obtained on the routine examination. Press the "TDI" button and position the cursor at the base of the ventricular septum at a point slightly below (towards the apex) the point where the atrial septum turns into the ventricular septum. Adjust the baseline to about the middle of the screen or to a position where all the waveforms can be clearly seen. The tracing looks a bit like an inverted mitral inflow tracing with E and A waves appearing below the baseline and one or more positive waves above the baseline. The two diastolic waves below the baseline are called "E prime"(E') and "A prime"(A') (to identify them as separate from E and A waves of the mitral inflow) and a single systolic "S wave" above the baseline. (You will note there are also some smaller waves however we won't worry about them at the moment). Record a few beats, freeze the screen and measure the peak E', A' and S wave and save a clip of your measurements. The values obtained are useful in the assessment of both diastolic and systolic left ventricular function and you will learn more about their use later. It is important to note at this point that some labs use the lateral part of the mitral annulus rather than the medial part to obtain these measurements so go with the flow and use which ever technique the lab you're working in uses.

Clip 40: Apical 3- Chamber view
From the four-chamber view rotate the probe clockwise until aorta comes into view. You should now have an image that contains the aorta, left ventricle, a portion of the left atrium and mitral valve. Look for wall motion abnormalities. Also, if you weren't able to get good V1 and V2 Doppler tracings in the apical 5-chamber view you can sometimes obtain them from this view. Clip a view of your efforts and than push the Color button. Look for mitral regurgitation or any flow disturbance within the left ventricle or along the left ventricular outflow tract. Clip a view of your "colourful" efforts.

Clip 41: Apical 2 - Chamber view
From the apical 3-chamber view, continue rotating the probe in a clockwise fashion until the aorta disappears and you have an image that contains only the left ventricle, left atrium and mitral valve. Look for left ventricular wall motion abnormalities - turn the colour on by pushing the Colour button and look for mitral regurgitation. Clip views of your efforts – one with the colour off and one with it on.

Subcostal views:

Place the probe under the xiphisternum with the light on the patient's right. You will have to increase the depth as well as adjust the probe's position by sliding left or right and rotating or angling the probe slightly to obtain the views indicated below.

Clip 42: Long axis view of the heart.
As indicated in Chapter 4, this view is similar to an apical 4-chamber view but from a different perspective. Make sure the aorta and aortic valve do not appear in the picture – if they do, you are angled too far anteriorly.

Sometimes subcostal views are the only views obtainable because parasternal and apical views are impossible. In such circumstances, many measurements can be done from this view. It is the preferred view for assessing the presence of right ventricular hypertrophy by measuring RV wall thickness and is occasionally useful for assessing eccentric tricuspid regurgitation and getting a better angle on the TR jet. You can also use it to measure LV wall thickness if you were not able to do it in the parasternal long.

Clip 43: Colour over atrial septum
Look for an ASD or any other evidence of shunting at the atrial level. Flow coming towards you (red) is usually, but not always, indicative of a shunt at the atrial level as blood flows from the more posterior left atrium into the more anterior right atrium. With large shunts, the diagnosis is seldom a problem, smaller shunts e.g. PFO's can be more challenging to find and can be diagnostically problematic. Flow from either the IVC or SVC may "bounce off" the atrial septum and get redirected anteriorly fooling you into thinking a shunt is present.

Clip 44: Short axis view-base:
From the long axis view, rotate the probe 90 degrees to produce the short axis view at the base of the heart (just as you did in the parasternal views). Here you can repeat and re-assess any and all measurements you made in

clips 17-23 especially if the parasternal views were difficult. Remember to use colour and Doppler as needed.

Clip 45: Short axis view mid-ventricular level
By angulating the probe towards apex, short-axis images of the ventricle will appear. If time and image quality permits you can even try to get all 3 cross section views of the ventricle at the mitral valve, mid-ventricular, and apical (or pseudoapical) levels much as you did in the parasternal views. Once again, you now have a second chance to acquire these views and look at ventricular function and abnormal wall motion.

Clip 46: IVC
Angulate the probe towards the patient's liver and find the IVC as it enters into the right atrium. Measure the diameter and show respiratory collapse by asking the patient to take a quick "sniff." You might consider doing this in two different clips, one for diameter and for the collapse with sniff. Some people will also show collapse with sniff by doing an M-mode through the IVC but this is not absolute necessary. Remember, you lose big points by recording the aorta and claiming it's a distended IVC!

Clip 47: Hepatic veins
Use colour Doppler to find a hepatic vein that is draining into the IVC. Usually the easiest one to find will be the left hepatic vein that enters the IVC just before the IVC enters the right atrium. If this hepatic vein appears to enter the right atrium directly, call your staff person – if you're proven to be correct, you will be praised effusively and automatically get a superior on your evaluation as you've just discovered a potentially important systemic venous anomaly!

Clip 48: Doppler of Hepatic Veins
With the colour Doppler on, push the cursor button and place the sample volume (the little box on the cursor) into the hepatic vein about 1 cm above where it enters the IVC and then hit the PW Doppler button. Adjust the baseline and the scale knobs so that the tracing is nicely centered and displayed on the screen. Mark the "S" "D" and "A" waves (systolic, diastolic which appear below the baseline and atrial wave which is a smaller wave appearing above the baseline) and any systolic reversal SR or diastolic reversal DR waves (these will also occur above the baseline). Identification of the various waves can be aided by timing with the ECG. You will note that these waves change in amplitude over the respiratory cycle. A respiratory marker can also be utilized on the screen should you so desire (details available from your friendly tech). Hepatic venous waveforms can

---

be used to diagnose constrictive pericarditis and restrictive cardiomyopathy amongst other things. They are however a challenge to get and accurately record – if you like bobbing for apples or playing whack-a-mole, you're going to love hepatic veins.

Suprasternal Views:

Place the probe just over the sternal notch with the light towards the chin. Remember the aorta runs from anterior to posterior and from the patients right to left. Slight angulation left or right or a bit of rotation is often necessary to visualize the aorta. Still can't see it? Try placing the probe in the right supraclavicular fossa. The aorta tends to dilate and unfold with age so keep this in mind as well when you are imaging older individuals.

Clip 49: Aorta
Often these views are very sub-optimal and while you may not see the aortic walls well on 2-D echo, a distinct flow will be seen with colour Doppler. The transverse portion of the aorta is usually best seen and atheroma can often be visualized. Clip a view of what you can find and then push the colour button. Red flow is usually from the ascending aorta or carotids or subclavian while blue flow is generally from the descending aorta, the SVC or innominate vein. Clip a view of the aorta with the colour on.

Clip 50: Doppler of the Descending Aorta
Place your cursor over the aorta and use CW Doppler to measure the velocities of the descending aorta. Look for any diastolic flow reversal (jet in diastole above the baseline), which might mean AI or a PDA. Also look for any coarctation pattern in the Doppler recording, which would be high systolic velocities (reflecting the pressure gradient) with continuous diastolic forward flow. This pattern is sometimes called the saw-tooth pattern.

Clip 51: The spider or crab view
Generally not part of the standard examination, and so it has been omitted here. Nevertheless keep in mind that some labs may use it at times.

And now you're done.

Go ice your shoulder and stretch a little.

However any abnormalities might require you to take extra pictures. For example if the patient actually has a VSD, you may need to calculate the gradient across the VSD. Also, if someone has significant MR you will need to quantify that to determine if it is mild, moderate, or severe. We'll talk about that more in the following chapter.

Authors Note:

An electronic version of this book is available on iTunes and contains moving echo clips for each description contained in this chapter.

Search for it on iTunes or Scan the QR code below

Review questions

1. Quantifying mitral regurgitation with colour flow doppler is best done in which view:
   a) Apical
   b) Parasternal long axis
   c) Parasternal short axis
   d) Subcostal

2. Measuring the LVOT diameter is done in which view:
   a) Apical
   b) Parasternal long axis
   c) Parasternal short axis
   d) Subcostal

Chapter 6 - Interpreting the Echo

In this Chapter:

- Ways to assess systolic dysfunction
- Ways to measure ejection fraction: volumetric and Simpson's method
- Describing wall motion abnormalities
- Assessing the severity of valvular disease
- Defining the terms: regurgitant volume, regurgitant fraction, and estimated regurgitant orifice (ERO)

Up until now, we've focused on how to perform an echo. Although the main focus of this book has always been to get you through that first stressful month of your echo rotation when you learn how to scan, this chapter will guide you through the preliminary analysis of your echo images. Sure you could just blindly clip images and measure everything I told you to measure but it's more important that you understand why these things are being done. It's all well and good to measure the waveforms in the pulmonary veins but unless you understand how it relates to diastolic dysfunction, it will all seem pretty meaningless and boring.

6.1 SYSTOLIC DYSFUNCTION

One of the most important things people want to know with an echo is, "What is the ejection fraction?" Knowing if someone has impaired systolic function is very important for both management and prognosis. There are many ways to estimate ejection fraction (EF), and some are better than others. The computer will calculate EF based on the left ventricular end-diastolic diameter (LVEDD) and left ventricular end-systolic diameter (LVESD) measurements you took with M-mode (Clip 10 from the previous chapter). It assumes the ventricle is an ellipse and therefore that end-diastolic volume is $(LVEDD)^3$ and that end-systolic volume is $(LVESD)^3$ and thus it is called the **volumetric method**. So the computer calculates EF as:

$$EF = \frac{(LVEDD)^3 - (LVESD)^3}{(LVEDD)^3}$$

As I said, this ejection fraction is generated automatically by the computer and will appear on your screen. However, you can appreciate that the assumption that the LV is a perfect ellipse is grossly flawed and this calculation is also very dependent on your M-mode measurements of the LV wall thickness and cavity size. Slight inaccuracies in the measurements can yield wild variations in ejection fraction and for the most part this number is not very accurate. This method also assumes that the LV contraction is symmetric, so in the presence of wall motion abnormalities it is invalid and should be ignored.

The **Simpson's method** or biplane method is another way to estimate EF. This technique requires the echocardiographer (i.e. you) to trace the endocardial border of the left ventricle in both systole and diastole in two different views (usually the apical 4-chamber and 2-chamber). The computer then divides the LV cavity into a number of discs and calculates the volume of each disk as if they were perfect cylinders. It then adds up the volume of all the discs to get the LV volume. It will repeat this in systole and diastole, and then use these volumes to calculate an ejection fraction. An example is shown in Figure 6.1, with the systolic and diastolic tracings superimposed.

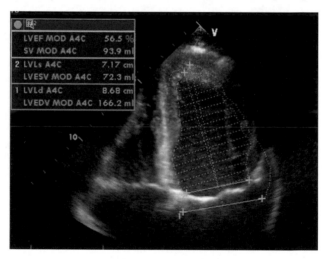

Figure 6.1: Simpson's method in the 4-chamber view
A similar tracing in 2-chamber view is needed for an EF to be calculated

The main drawback of this method is that it requires very good quality images where the endocardial border is clearly seen, which is not always the case. Finally, it is somewhat time consuming to trace out the endocardial border four separate times. For these reasons, even if this is one of the better methods not everyone uses it all the time.

The "eye ball" method is probably the most ubiquitous method out there but not something you should be depending on early on. You really need to have looked at upwards of a hundred echos before you can reliably start estimating ejection fraction just by the appearance of the left ventricle. That being said, if there are no wall motion abnormalities and all segments are contracting normally, then you can confidently say that the ejection fraction is normal.

Finally, a good way to assess EF when you're first starting out is to base yourself on wall motion. In order so that everyone can speak the same language, the LV was divided into 16 (or 17 depending on who you talk to) segments and each segment given a precise name (see below). First it was sliced into 3 cross sections at the base of the heart, at the mid-ventricular level, and at the apex. Not by chance, these 3 cross sections correspond to the 3 echocardiographic short axis views of the LV (mitral valve, papillary muscles, and apex). Each of these cross sections was then divided into six sections, except for the apical cut which was divided into four. Finally, the apical tip makes up the 17th segment, although since the apical tip is not always visible, some limit themselves to analyzing the 16 segments.

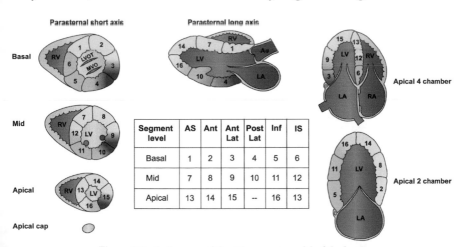

Segment level	AS	Ant	Ant Lat	Post Lat	Inf	IS
Basal	1	2	3	4	5	6
Mid	7	8	9	10	11	12
Apical	13	14	15	--	16	13

Figure 6.2: A diagram of the 16 segment model of the heart
AS=anteroseptal, Ant=anterior, Lat=lateral, Post=posterior, Inf=inferior, IS=inferoseptal

Each segment should be assessed as you proceed through your echo clips and then double checked since you can see each segment in multiple views. A segment should contract and thicken by >50%. Anything that thickens by less than 50% is termed **hypokinetic**. A segment that doesn't thicken at all is termed **akinetic**. It's important to note that wall segments may move as they are "dragged" along by adjacent normal segments but if they don't thicken, then they are truly akinetic. A **dyskinetic** segment means that it actually moves out as the rest of the segments are moving in during contraction and an **aneurysmal** segment is exactly what its name implies – an aneurysm.

After you've counted up all your segments, some simple math will give you a pretty good assessment of the ejection fraction. Start by assigning one point to all normal segments, a half-point to all hypokinetic segments, and zero points to akinetic segments. Then add up the total and divide by 16 (or 17 if you have a good view of the apical cap) and multiply by a normal ejection fraction, say 60%. Here's a practical example. Let's say that post MI somebody has inferior and septal wall motion abnormalities, such that there are two hypokinetic segments and two akinetic segments. Assume you can't see the apical cap. If you add up all the segments you have 12 normal segments for 12 points, 2 hypokinetic segments for 1 point, and 0 points for the akinetic segments. That would give you a total score of 13/16. Multiply that by a normal EF of 60% and you get 48.75%. Thus you can safely estimate that the EF post MI is 45-50%. Here is the formula in condensed form:

$$\frac{\text{Total wall segment score}}{\text{\# of segments assessed}} \times \text{Normal EF} = \text{Calculated EF}$$

This method may seem time consuming, but it will help you practice assessing wall motion and is much more reliable in your early days of echo training when your "eyeball" isn't fully calibrated yet. One word or warning though; you may come across something called the wall motion score index (WMSI) which is a completely different animal. Although the basic idea is the same, it scores the segments differently and is not very useful in assessing ejection fraction. So don't get the two confused.

6.2 VALVULAR DISEASE

Assessing the presence of valvular disease is also critically important when interpreting the echo. As previously noted, some degree of regurgitation may be normal and not clinically significant. Remember that we can measure PA pressures only because almost everyone has some TR. Nevertheless, it is important to characterize and describe any valve problems that you see. I've mentioned that you should be looking for regurgitation any time you put colour on a valve, but how do you decide if it's mild, moderate or severe? Many experienced echocardiographers will use the "eye ball" method once again. They can confidently and fairly reliably say, "That looks trivial or mild" or "That's at least moderate." Although you will one day gain that ability yourself, to start off we will quickly review how to characterize these lesions as mild, moderate, or severe.

Included below is a summary from the 2006 ACC/AHA guidelines on valve disease. They offer up a comprehensive and to the point summary of how to classify valvular disease. As you notice, they don't mention much about right-sided lesions probably because they're fairly rare in the non-congenital setting and in most adults are not terribly clinically significant.

Parameter	Aortic Stenosis		
	Mild	Moderate	Severe
Jet velocity (m/s)	<3.0	3.0-4.0	>4.0
Mean gradient (mmHg)	<25	25-40	>40
Valve area (cm^2)	>1.5	1.0-1.5	<1.0
V1/V2			<0.25

Parameter	Mitral Stenosis*		
	Mild	Severe	Very Severe
Mean Gradient (mmHg)	<5	5-10	>10
Pulmonary Artery systolic pressure (mmHg)	<30	30-50	>50
Valve area (cm^2)	>1.5	1.0-1.5	<1.0

Parameter	Aortic Regurgitation		
	Mild	Moderate	Severe
Vena contracta (cm)	<0.3	0.3-0.6	>0.6
Color jet width (% of LVOT)	<25%	25-60%	>65%
Regurgitant volume (ml)	<30ml	30-60	>60
Regurgitant fraction (%)	<30	30-50	>50
Estimated Regurgitant Orifice (cm^2)	<0.1	0.1-0.3	>0.3

Parameter	Mitral regurgitation		
	Mild	Moderate	Severe
Ventra contracta (cm)	<0.3	0.3-0.7	>0.7
Regurgitant volume (ml)	<30	30-60	>60
Regurgitant fraction (ml)	<30	30-50	>50
Estimated Regurgitant Orifice (cm^2)	<0.2	0.2-0.4	>0.4

Table 6.1: Assessing the severity of valvular lesions

*In the 2014 guidelines the classification of mitral stenosis was renamed. Moderate disease became severe and severe disease became very severe

In 2014, the guidelines moved towards an ABCD classification scheme.

Stage	Official definition	My definition
Stage A	At risk	Patients with risk factors for developing valve disease
Stage B	Progressive	Patients that were previously called mild or moderate
Stage C	Asymptomatic Severe	Severe but no symptoms
Stage D	Symptomatic Severe	Severe but has symptoms

I have nevertheless opted to present the 2006 table to you, purely for educational purposes, since I believe it is easier to understand. However, you should ultimately adopt the new naming structure unless of course it is changed again in newer guidelines.

Aortic stenosis is a fairly important valve lesion and you should memorize what characterizes severe AS, as it will come up frequently in both clinical settings and on exams. The jet velocity, mean gradient, and valve area are calculated routinely on every echo so you will have plenty of opportunity to become familiar with the numbers.

Mitral stenosis is not seen as frequently as it once was now that rheumatic fever is less common, however you will still see it often enough that it is worthwhile becoming familiar with the numbers. We don't routinely calculate the mitral valve area unless we suspect stenosis. Sometimes though you will see a mitral valve with the typical hockey stick deformity and suspect MS. If you do, it may be worthwhile to trace a Velocity Time Integral of the mitral inflow pattern (in CW). This will give you the gradients and allow you to calculate the valve area by using the continuity equation, as we did for AS in Chapter 3. (Bear in mind that the continuity equation only works here if there is no mitral regurgitation) You should read the chapter again if you need a quick refresher of how to do this.

In brief: A_2 is the mitral valve area you're trying to calculate, V_2 is the VTI of the mitral inflow, A_1 is the area of the LVOT, and V_1 is the VTI of the LVOT. You can also use Pressure Half Time to estimate mitral valve area (MVA), where: $MVA = 220/PHT$ but more on that in Chapter 7.

Aortic and mitral regurgitation are often assessed qualitatively (which is fancy way to say the eye ball method) based on the size of the regurgitant jet seen on colour flow Doppler. There are also quantitative criteria for the regurgitant valve lesions that deserve a brief mention. **Vena contracta** is essentially the narrowest neck of a regurgitant jet. Measuring it requires nothing more involved that using the calipers on the echo machine to measure the width of the jet at that narrowest point. An example of the vena contracta of an AI jet is shown below. The narrowest portion is shown between the two short arrows and labeled VC.

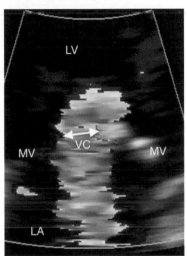

Figure 6.3: Measurement of vena contracta

Another new concept is regurgitant volume and regurgitant fraction. **Regurgitant volume** is simply the amount of blood in ml that is regurgitated back across the incompetent valve with each heartbeat. The **regurgitant fraction** in mitral regurgitation is simply the regurgitant volume divided by the mitral inflow volume, in effect the percentage of the blood volume that is regurgitated backwards. It can be calculated easily enough by:

Regurgitant fraction = Regurgitant volume / Volume of mitral inflow x 100%

Both regurgitant volume and regurgitant fraction can be calculated using the continuity equation, however we will delay going over the math until the next and final chapter.

The **estimated regurgitant orifice** (ERO) is essentially the area through which the regurgitation is occurring. It is calculated using the proximal isovelocity surface area (PISA) method. It too is simply a derivation of the continuity equation.

All these techniques are used sparingly as the math can become cumbersome. We will review these more advanced formulae and other topics in the final chapter. For now, suffice it to say that there are both qualitative and quantitative ways to assess valve lesions.

Now let's summarize what we've gone over in this chapter:

- There are a number of ways to assess EF: the volumetric method, Simpson's method, the eyeball method, and the wall motion method.

- The volumetric method uses the ventricular diameters in systole and diastole, measured in M-mode, and assumes the LV is a perfect ellipse.

- Simpson's method involves tracing the endocardial border in systole and diastole and dividing the ventricle into a series of discs in order to estimate end-diastolic and end-systolic volume.

- Wall motion can be assessed by dividing the LV into 16 distinct segments and classifying each one as normal, hypokinetic, akinetic, dyskinetic or aneurysmal.

- Valvular disease should be characterized as mild, moderate or severe using both qualitative and quantitative parameters.

- Vena contracta is the width of the narrowest neck of a regurgitant jet.

- Regurgitant volume is the volume of blood passing back through the leaky valve.

- Regurgitant fraction is the regurgitant volume divided by total flow.

Review questions

1. In a 16 segment model of the heart, if 4 segments are hypokinetic and 2 segments are akinetic, then the projected EF should be approximately (assuming a normal EF is 60%):
   a) 35%
   b) 40%
   c) 45%
   d) 50%

2. Which of the following valve lesions is severe:

   a) Mean gradient across the aortic valve of 35mmHg
   b) Mean gradient across the mitral valve of 12mmHg
   c) Aortic valve area of 1.2 cm^2
   d) Mitral valve area of 2.0 cm^2

Chapter 7 - Advanced Topics

In this Chapter:
- Measuring cardiac output
- Assessing diastolic dysfunction
- Pressure Half-Time
- Regurgitant volume and regurgitant fraction
- PISA and estimated regurgitant orifice (ERO)

As we begin the final chapter, it is important to remember that this book was always intended to be an introductory manual of echocardiography; something that would be read and one day outgrown in favour of more comprehensive texts. Nevertheless, included in this chapter are several "advanced" topics. The main point of the discussion here is to introduce you to these topics so that later you can read up on them in more depth once you have gained more experience.

7.1 CARDIAC OUTPUT

Although not something that is looked at routinely, it is possible to assess cardiac output (CO) using echo. Remember that cardiac output is heart rate (HR) times stroke volume (SV). We can use the continuity equation to figure out the stroke volume which is really the amount of blood being ejected across the open aortic valve, which is none other than A_1 x VTI_1.

$$SV = A_1 \times VTI_1$$

A_1 being the LVOT area and VTI_1 being the trace of the LVOT jet. As you can see, these are values you measure routinely with every echo and the computer will in fact automatically calculate stroke volume every time you measure these values.

Now all that remains is the heart rate, since: $CO = SV \times HR$

After you trace the LVOT jet, you then move your cursor over to the next jet. Essentially here you're measuring the R-R interval. The computer takes the reciprocal of that, multiplies it by 60, and suddenly you have a heart rate. So once you trace your LVOT and measure your R-R interval, the computer will take all that information and give you a cardiac output. Of course that assumes your heart rate is regular. If you have an irregular heartbeat, all bets are off. Also small discrepancies in measuring the LVOT diameter can lead to large differences in calculating LVOT area and thus stroke volume. Due to all these potential sources of error, we generally don't look at measures of cardiac output on echo even though it does come up automatically.

7.2 PRESSURE HALF TIME (PHT)

Pressure half time is an interesting physiologic principle and is useful for assessing the severity of valvular lesions, mitral stenosis in particular. Remember that blood flows only so long as a pressure difference exists between cardiac chambers. Once pressure equalizes, blood flow stops and the valves close. The time it takes for the pressure to equalize is important. In stenotic lesions (like MS) this time is extended. In regurgitant lesions (like AI) this is reduced. The way to gage this variation is to use what is called the **pressure half time**. As the name implies, pressure half time is the time it takes for the pressure difference to fall by 50% (sort of like using a half-life in physics or biology). Since we can't measure pressure directly, we rely once again on the Bernoulli equation. With some quick math we find that a drop in pressure by 50% means that velocity has to fall to 70% of its maximal level. So when you measure a pressure half time by drawing a slope along the velocity jet that you measured with your Doppler probe, the computer is figuring out when you reach 70% of your maximum velocity, calculating that it means 50% of your pressure, and measuring the time from maximum velocity to that point. This time interval is your pressure half time. A good formula to remember is that for mitral stenosis the mitral valve area (MVA) = 220 / PHT. The number 220 was empirically derived and simply has to be memorized, there's nothing magical about it. Keep in mind though, that the 220 number only works for native mitral valves. It's not valid for anyone with a mitral prosthesis.

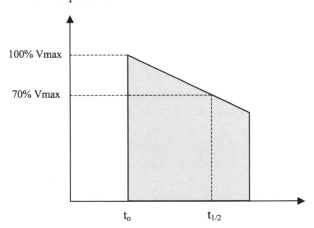

Figure 7.1: Example of pressure half time

There is perhaps no more hotly debated topic in echocardiography today then how to measure diastolic dysfunction, or the impaired relaxation of the heart. To grossly oversimplify an incredibly complex topic, we go back to the Doppler waveform of the mitral inflow. The ventricle does most of its filling early in diastole (that's the E wave) and then again when the atrium contracts (that's the A wave). Normally, the E wave is much larger than the A wave because the atrium contributes little to ventricular filling. In stage 1 diastolic dysfunction or **impaired relaxation**, the ventricle becomes stiff and harder to fill, and the atrium plays a progressively larger role in ventricular filling.

In stage II diastolic dysfunction or **pseudonormalization,** things get worse and worse. Left atrial pressure and wedge pressure rise. As a result, more of the ventricular filling can occur passively because the filling pressures have gone up so the E wave once again becomes larger than the A wave. So, the mitral inflow pattern looks similar to normal, hence the name pseudonormalization. Stage III and stage IV will show a continuation of this process with most LV filling occurring early but not lasting very long (because pressures quickly equalize) resulting in very tall but very narrow E waves with almost absent A waves.

How does one tell these different stages apart, especially since stage II is essentially normal looking? In the past, people used to use the pulmonary veins to differentiate the stages. However, more recently people have turned to tissue Doppler. Remember tissue Doppler measures the velocity of whatever part of the myocardium the focus of the cursor is placed on. The left ventricle will have three major movements: one in systole (the S wave or positive deflection), one in early diastole as it actively relaxes (the E′ wave and first negative deflection) and the last in late diastole after the atrium contracts (the A′ wave and second negative deflection which will occur after the p wave on the ECG tracing). As you can see the tissue Doppler waves mirror and the mitral inflow waves and they are actually inverses of one another. Normally E′ is larger than A′. However, as diastolic dysfunction develops the A′ wave becomes progressively larger than the E′ wave. So one way to differentiate normal from pseudonormal is to look at the tissue Doppler tracings and see if E′ is normal or decreased. One other thing to look at is the E/ E′ ratio. As diastolic dysfunction worsens, this ratio gets larger and larger. When it is larger than 15 it suggests high filling pressures and an elevated LVEDP. (This ratio has actually recently been called into question by some published reports, but I would stick with it for now.)

Diastolic dysfunction is a very complicated topic and I don't expect that you've absorbed much of what is written here. However, Table 7.1 summarizes key measures in diastolic dysfunction. I recommend using it when you start out, to keep all these measurements straight in your head.

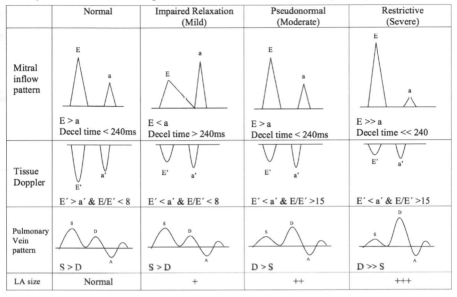

	Normal	Impaired Relaxation (Mild)	Pseudonormal (Moderate)	Restrictive (Severe)
Mitral inflow pattern	E > a Decel time < 240ms	E < a Decel time > 240ms	E > a Decel time < 240ms	E >> a Decel time << 240
Tissue Doppler	E' > a' & E/E' < 8	E' < a' & E/E' < 8	E' < a' & E/E' >15	E' < a' & E/E' >15
Pulmonary Vein pattern	S > D	S > D	D > S	D >> S
LA size	Normal	+	++	+++

Table 7.1: Classification of diastolic dysfunction

7.4 REGURGITANT VOLUME AND REGURGITANT FRACTION

In the previous chapter we introduced the concepts of regurgitant volume and regurgitant fraction. They can be calculated fairly easily by using a variation of the continuity equation. Remember that everything that goes into the LV must come out. So assuming no shunt:

Volume of mitral inflow = Volume through LVOT + regurgitant volume of MR

The volume of blood being ejected through the LVOT is really just the stroke volume and we've already covered how to calculate that (it's the VTI of the LVOT times the LVOT area). The volume of mitral inflow can be calculated based on the same principle and all you need is the VTI of mitral inflow (measured in CW) and the area of the mitral valve which can be calculated the same way you calculate the LVOT; by measuring the diameter of the valve annulus and then using πr^2 to calculate the area. So after some re-arranging:

Regurgitant volume of MR = Volume of mitral inflow − volume through LVOT

Regurgitant volume of MR = VTI_{MV} x $Area_{MV}$ − VTI_{LVOT} x $Area_{LVOT}$

Regurgitant volume of MR = VTI_{MV} x $\pi(D_{MV}/2)^2$ − VTI_{LVOT} x $\pi(D_{LVOT}/2)^2$

Although the equation seems daunting, once you understand the basic principles, you can see that it is really just an expansion of the continuity equation.

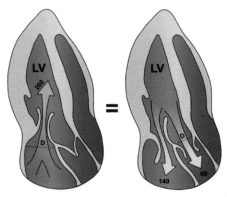

Figure 7.2: How to calculate regurgitant volume

In the example above, the mitral valve inflow is 200ml while outflow through the aortic valve is only 60ml. Thus the regurgitant volume is 140ml.

The **regurgitant fraction** will be much simpler to explain. It is simply the regurgitant volume divided by the mitral inflow volume, in effect the percentage of the blood volume that is regurgitated backwards. It can be calculated easily enough by:

Regurgitant fraction = Regurgitant volume / Volume of mitral inflow x 100%

In the above case, it will be 140/200 = 70%. Although the formulas are convoluted, the math is fairly straightforward. If you can calculate the area of a circle, you're set. The biggest problem here is something we've mentioned before. Mess up the LVOT or mitral valve annulus diameter, even by a little bit, and your numbers will be way off which is why these measurements are not done very often.

Finally, the **estimated regurgitant orifice area** (ERO) is also used in some circumstances to quantify the degree of MR (and to a lesser degree AI). It is based on a concept called PISA (proximal isovelocity surface area). PISA is initially quite complicated to understand. If we take MR as an example again, imagine the blood that is flowing backwards from the LV to the LA. As the blood flows towards the defect in the mitral valve (whether it's a prolapsed leaflet, mal-coaptation, or whatever) the blood will accelerate. Since blood is coming from all directions towards this opening in the normally closed mitral valve, there is essentially this dome shaped area where all the blood is flowing towards the valve at the same velocity. On echo, with colour flow, what you will see is a semi-circle that is entirely the same colour. Hence, all the blood within that semicircular *surface area* which is *proximal* to the valve will have the same velocity, or *isovelocity*. This is simply a physical property of fluid flowing through a drain, and is common to the blood in your heart and the water in your bathtub. Fortunately, we can use this fluidic eccentricity to measure MR. Once again, we will rely on the good old continuity equation and define our variables. Since the blood flowing in through the PISA must equal the amount of blood flowing out the other side of the mitral valve into the LA we can say that:

$$\text{PISA flow} = \text{MR flow}$$

Area of the PISA hemisphere x velocity in the PISA hemisphere = ERO x VTI_{MR}

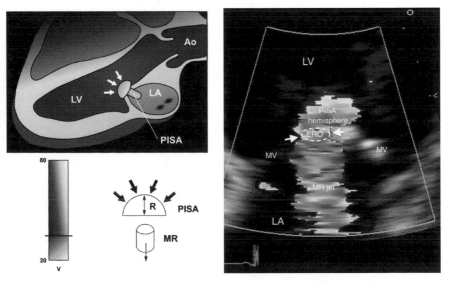

Figure 7.3: The elements involved in calculation of a ERO using PISA

Here we are trying to solve for ERO. The VTI of the MR jet is easily measurable with CW Doppler. The area of the PISA hemisphere is easy enough to calculate because all you need is the radius of that circle and a working knowledge of high school geometry ($A=2\pi r^2$, remember that you're calculating the surface area of a sphere, not a circle). The velocity of the PISA hemisphere is more complicated. Here you actually need to adjust something called the aliasing velocity, which is the velocity of the colour flow Doppler. Normally, the colour map is set so that both the red and blue aliasing velocities are equal. However, you can manually change this. When measuring a PISA, you must do exactly that and adjust the aliasing velocities until the PISA semicircle is regular and a uniform colour. If you left the aliasing velocities as they were, the shape of that semi-circle would actually not be circular and something closer to an amorphous blob. So you adjust the aliasing velocity until you see as near to perfect a semicircle as you can get, and that aliasing velocity is your PISA velocity (20 in the example above). Once again, by using the continuity equation and plugging in your three variables, you will be able to solve for the value you are looking for.

We've covered quite a few more advanced topics in this chapter with some rather complex formulas. In actuality though, you won't need to actually calculate any of these values with pen and paper. There are options in the menu that will calculate these values for you with the appropriate inputs. Just like the computer will automatically give you an aortic valve area after you trace V1 and V2 and measure an LVOT diameter, the computer will calculate a regurgitant volume or mitral valve area once you select that option from the menu and measure all the necessary components. So memorizing these formulas is not crucial but as you've seen they are all extrapolations of the continuity equation and can easily be derived if you understand the physiology and the physics that underlie them.

Also, it's important to look globally at what's going on with the heart. MR is likely to be important if someone has a dilated LA with pulmonary hypertension. Likewise with AI if the left ventricle is dilated with a reduced ejection fraction. When approaching a problem like this, don't miss the forest for the trees.

Now let's summarize what we've covered in this chapter:

- Stroke volume can be calculated by $Area_{LVOT}$ x VTI_{LVOT}. By calculating the heart rate, we can also estimate cardiac output by echo since CO = HR x SV
- Pressure half time (PHT) is the time it takes for pressure to decrease by 50% (or velocity to decrease by 70%) across a valve.
- Pressure half time is shortened in regurgitant lesions and lengthened in stenotic lesions
- Mitral valve area can be estimated with the formula
  Mitral valve area (MVA) = 220 / PHT
- Diastolic dysfunction can be assessed through changes in the E and A waves of the mitral inflow doppler signal. The E' and A' waves of tissue Doppler are also used in the assessment as is the pulmonary vein pattern.
- Regurgitant volume of MR = VTI_{MV} x $Area_{MV}$ – VTI_{LVOT} x $Area_{LVOT}$
- Regurgitant fraction of MR = Regurgitant volume/MV inflow volume x 100%
- The estimated regurgitant orifice (ERO) is assessed using the PISA method
- ERO = $2\pi r^2$ x aliasing velocity / VTI_{MR}

Review questions

1. If on mitral valve inflow E>a, and on tissue doppler the E/E´ ratio is <8, then this characterizes:
   a) Normal diastolic function
   b) Impaired relaxation (Grade 1)
   c) Pseudonormal function (Grade 2)
   d) Restriction (Grade 3)

2. A pressure half time of 110ms, implies that the mitral valve area is:

   a) 1 cm^2
   b) 1.5 cm^2
   c) 2 cm^2
   d) 2.5 cm^2

Final Thoughts

Echocardiography is one of those things that can seem very simple and yet be deceptively complicated. The physics behind it and the technology involved in constructing an echo machine is staggering when you stop and think about it. The math can be mind numbing and the formulae can drive you to drink.

The only solution is to start from base principles and build yourself up. In reality, you just need two remember two formulae: the Bernoulli and the Continuity equation. Everything else is just a derivation of those two. There may be up to 50 echo clips per study, but there are really just 5 views: parasternal long, parasternal short, apical, subcostal, and suprasternal. The number of things you need to measure and analyze may seem endless but ultimately you only have four valves and four chambers to worry about. As with all things in life, approach it systematically and soon what once seemed complicated will become routine.

There is no substitute for holding the probe in your hand and scanning patients yourself. This can be difficult in a busy lab where things are often rushed. In that case, I would suggest finding a good friend and taking turns scanning each other over lunch or at the end of the day. Although, it may seem like a ridiculous thing to do, you need to log the hours to gain proficiency. There is no other way.

You should soon graduate to one of the other textbooks I mentioned at the beginning, and then you will see how versatile (and how complicated) echo can be. But for now, my hope is that this book has provided you with the road map you need to get started.

Best wishes in your training.

Christopher Labos MD, CM FRCPC

Appendix:
Answers to review questions

<u>Chapter 1</u> 1. B 2. A	<u>Chapter 5</u> 1. A 2. B
<u>Chapter 2</u> 1. B 2. A	<u>Chapter 6</u> 1. C 2. B
<u>Chapter 3</u> 1. A 2. C 3. A	<u>Chapter 7</u> 1. A 2. C
<u>Chapter 4</u> 1. B 2. C 3. D	